Love, God, and the Art of French Cooking

ALSO BY JAMES F. TWYMAN

Books

The Art of Spiritual Peacemaking
The Barn Dance*
Emissary of Light
Emissary of Love
The Kabbalah Code (with Philip Gruber)*
Messages from Thomas
The Moses Code*
The Prayer of St. Francis
Praying Peace
The Proof (with Anakha Coman)*
The Proposing Tree
The Secret of the Beloved Disciple
Ten Spiritual Lessons I Learned at the Mall

Films

Indigo
The Indigo Evolution
Into Me See
The Moses Code: The Movie*
The Proof

Music

Ecclesia
Emissary of Light
For the Beloved
God Has No Religion
May Peace Prevail on Earth
The Moses Code Frequency Meditation*
The Order of the Beloved Disciple
12 Prayers

*Available from Hay House

Please visit:

Hay House UK: **www.hayhouse.co.uk**
Hay House USA: **www.hayhouse.com**®
Hay House Australia: **www.hayhouse.com.au**
Hay House South Africa: **www.hayhouse.co.za**
Hay House India: **www.hayhouse.co.in**

Love, God, and the Art of French Cooking

James F. Twyman

HAY HOUSE, INC.

Carlsbad, California • New York City
London • Sydney • Johannesburg
Vancouver • Hong Kong • New Delhi

First published and distributed in the United Kingdom by:
Hay House UK Ltd, 292B Kensal Rd, London W10 5BE. Tel.: (44) 20 8962 1230;
Fax: (44) 20 8962 1239. www.hayhouse.co.uk

Published and distributed in the United States of America by:
Hay House, Inc., PO Box 5100, Carlsbad, CA 92018-5100. Tel.: (1) 760 431 7695 or
(800) 654 5126; Fax: (1) 760 431 6948 or (800) 650 5115. www.hayhouse.com

Published and distributed in Australia by:
Hay House Australia Ltd, 18/36 Ralph St, Alexandria NSW 2015. Tel.: (61) 2 9669
4299; Fax: (61) 2 9669 4144. www.hayhouse.com.au

Published and distributed in the Republic of South Africa by:
Hay House SA (Pty), Ltd, PO Box 990, Witkoppen 2068. Tel./Fax: (27) 11 467 8904.
www.hayhouse.co.za

Published and distributed in India by:
Hay House Publishers India, Muskaan Complex, Plot No.3, B-2, Vasant Kunj, New
Delhi – 110 070. Tel.: (91) 11 4176 1620; Fax: (91) 11 4176 1630.
www.hayhouse.co.in

Distributed in Canada by:
Raincoast, 9050 Shaughnessy St, Vancouver, BC V6P 6E5. Tel.: (1) 604 323 7100;
Fax: (1) 604 323 2600

Copyright © 2011 by James F. Twyman

The moral rights of the author have been asserted.

Editorial supervision: Jill Kramer • *Project editor:* Lisa Mitchell
Cover design: Amy Rose Grigoriou • *Interior design:* Nick C. Welch

Some names and identifying details have been changed to protect the
privacy of the individuals involved.

The author of this book does not dispense medical advice or prescribe the use of
any technique as a form of treatment for physical or medical problems without
the advice of a physician, either directly or indirectly. The intent of the author is
only to offer information of a general nature to help you in your quest for emotional and spiritual wellbeing. In the event you use any of the information in this
book for yourself, which is your constitutional right, the author and the publisher
assume no responsibility for your actions.

A catalogue record for this book is available from the British Library.

ISBN 978-1-84850-553-7

Printed and bound in Great Britain by CPI Group (UK) Ltd, Croydon, CR0 4YY.

To my mother—
the first person to teach
me about the love of food.

Contents

"There is no love sincerer than the love of food."

— GEORGE BERNARD SHAW

"Eating unloved food is like living an unloved life."

— ROGER DUFAU

Introduction

When I was a child, I would watch my mother cook with great admiration. Even after I left home and entered adulthood, I claimed that she made the best lasagna in the world and that her taco salad was unmatched. While I was attending Loyola University and enjoying my share of Chicago-style pizza and a variety of other local favorites, nothing seemed to come close to the energy I felt around my family's dining table—especially when my mom pulled that steaming casserole dish out of the oven and I knew what magic lay beneath the tinfoil. The melted cheeses and other decadent ingredients may not have been the healthiest things for us at the time, but nothing could compare to the effect those meals had on my spirit, even to this day. As far as I was concerned, no worthy competition existed. Mom's cooking was the best.

Looking back I realized that there was another explanation for my feelings. Although my mom's food made an unmistakable impact on me personally, I'm sure there were others who were better cooks, but there was something very special happening in our kitchen that no one else could match—not the greatest chef in the world. Mom loved the whole family immensely, and that love seeped into her dishes like a fine fragrance that shifts the energy of an entire room. We could taste it, and it permeated our bodies with such eloquence that it didn't matter whose lasagna was better. It was the first time I realized that love has the power to transform food. A great dish is as much about the person preparing it as it is about the recipe itself.

These days it's my twenty-five-year-old daughter, Angela, who performs the same magic trick. Now and then when I'm lucky, she shows up at my home in Portland carrying a plate of one thing or another, and it never seems to last long before being devoured. She inherited a number of recipes from her grandmother, and those are the ones she usually likes to deliver—maybe because she knows how much I love them or because she realizes that her dad can't cook worth a lick.

If I took the time to figure out how much I spend eating at restaurants each year, it would be frightening . . . so it's always a welcome surprise when I see Angela standing on my porch, smiling, and holding a dish that came straight from her oven. Once again, love is the key, and I can taste it in every bite.

Maybe there's a part of me that doesn't want to learn the art of cooking myself because I'm afraid that the "daughter delivery service" might end if I do. Or perhaps there's a deeper reason I'm only now beginning to understand . . . and it is that richer meaning I seek and wish to share with you.

We experience so many synchronicities in our lives—brief encounters and events that have the potential to transform us. But these moments are often missed or disregarded; we are too busy and too harried, or perhaps too fearful of what we may discover about ourselves to embrace the experience. Sometimes, however, when we slow down (or are forced to slow down), we can finally see the incredible opportunities and flashes of insight that are available to us.

I talk about opening up and seizing the moment, but I'm no different from most people. And my moment, my brush with destiny, arrived with such suddenness that it was nearly impossible to miss. . . .

This book is about that fateful moment, and many others that followed, which you will read about. It happens to all of us at one point or another—the casino wheel spins and our number isn't called, and we realize it's time to pay a debt we've been ignoring for years. If we're lucky, the dreadful experience is also accompanied by the presence of someone who helps us look at the calamity from a different viewpoint, such as Clarence in *It's A Wonderful Life,* the angel who helped George Bailey (Jimmy Stewart's character) see that in spite of all his perceived failings, his life was really incredible—irreplaceable, in fact. The problem is that angels rarely announce themselves, usually because they don't realize that this is the role they've been given to play.

Maybe *you* have played the part of an angel for someone in your life—a friend who had reached the end of his or her rope, for example, and needed the wisdom only you could offer. Perhaps you said something that seemed unimportant at the time, but your words seeped effortlessly into this person's consciousness and were life changing. Who knows? Angels show up in more ways than we could ever guess, and that's the beauty of it. It's the disguise that makes the whole thing work.

It was while writing this story that I learned even greater lessons—the ones that slid past my consciousness when they were happening but which ripened during the subsequent days and weeks. I thought one particular lesson was the key, but then others presented themselves—lessons that I intuitively knew weren't just meant for me.

You'll probably relate to much of what you're about to read, for we have all traversed these paths and lonely roads . . . and have the blisters to show for it. One thing I know for sure is that I am a better man for it, and although the lessons were often seared into my soul like branding the hide of a prized bull, at least the mark is permanent. No matter what happens, I can look down at the raised flesh and say, "God bless you, cursed wound . . . and thanks for the memories."

Roger Dufau, master chef and mystic

The following story is true. I did change the names of some of the main "characters" to ensure their privacy, but Roger, whom you will get to know well, is very real indeed. Many of the conversations you'll read were actually recorded so that I could represent his philosophy as accurately as possible, while others have been slightly reconstituted for the sake of the story. Overall, though, this is about as real as it gets, especially what I went through to get to the finish line. Now that I'm here, I can't think of anything I would rather share since I believe it's one of the most important lessons any of us can learn.

So sit down with a glass of good wine and a few slices of French cheese. They'll put you in the right mood for sure.

CHAPTER ONE

Abandoned

The final look said it all. As the car backed out of the driveway and the morning sun lit the left side of Michele's face, I knew it was over. That *we* were over. Our eyes met for a second, and then hers shifted to the rearview mirror. I stood there wishing she would glance at me again, one final look to give me some kind of hope. But she didn't. A moment later the car turned left onto Mill Street and was gone. It was 7 A.M., and the day was already off to a terrible start.

I'm not really sure how long I stood there staring in the direction she drove. Her car had disappeared and others were moving in both directions . . . heading to workplaces, dropping children off at school. They all seemed to have a purpose, as if they knew where they were going and why they were there. I, on the other hand, was suddenly stuck without a car in a country that seemed remarkably similar to my own, but was not. I barely knew where I was and definitely had no idea where I was going.

It was early November. My lady friend, Michele, had come up with the idea of spending a few days together in Elora, a tiny hamlet an hour outside of Toronto. I flew there from my home in Oregon with high hopes of us making a genuine connection, the sort that might even survive the distance and long hours of travel. In the end, though, the reason Michele left had nothing to do with how many miles separated us. She told me that I was too liberal and she was too conservative, which made no sense to me. She believed in straight lines, while mine were dotted or curved, she said. That led to an argument, and before long we were lying on opposite sides of the bed, doing whatever we could to avoid accidental contact.

It felt as if a river was suddenly running between us, and no matter how hard I tried, I couldn't come up with the words to build a bridge to bring us back to the same side. I reached out to touch her, and she moved away. She was already gone, even though she was only twelve inches from where I was lying.

Neither one of us slept much that night, as if we were hoping that the cool country air and dark sky might inspire something that we were unable to see or sense on our own. Perhaps there was a solution that was still invisible to the naked eye, one in which differences fade and the passion we felt months earlier would be reignited . . . *if only long enough to get me a ride to the airport*, I thought to myself.

Instead, early the next morning I was left standing in a gravel driveway at a bed-and-breakfast that was light-years from where I thought I needed to be. *What had I done to deserve this?* The sun's rays were clearing a straight path through the clouds, while my spirit could not have been more leveled.

It was the sound that first caught my attention—that distinct groan of hinges needing to be oiled. I turned to my right just as the screen door swung open and a pot of water came flying in my direction. A tall, distinguished-looking man glanced up at me, surprised to see anyone standing so close. Roger (pronounced in French as "Row-zhay"), is the co-owner of Drew House, along with his wife, Kathleen. We'd met the previous day when Michele and I checked in, but I hadn't seen either of them since. Later that night we found a restaurant that seemed sensible enough, and it was there that the seeds of our destruction were planted. By the time we returned to our room, they were in full blossom; and the only thing left was the great harvest, which finally and resolutely took place the next morning.

I was alone, and the man with his hair pulled back in a ponytail had nearly capped off the experience by baptizing me with dirty dishwater.

"Oh! I didn't see you there," Roger said in his thick French accent.

Not only is he the proprietor of Drew House, one of the most charming European-styled B&Bs in North America, but he is also a renowned chef, having owned fine restaurants in France, Toronto, and Australia. In Elora he's a minor celebrity, which is just as much a tribute to his cheerful, passionate demeanor as it is to his prowess in the kitchen.

Kathleen would later tell me a story that explained this better, especially in regard to the effect Roger had on many of the local women. He had overheard a group of them speaking in hushed tones and wondered what they meant by a certain word they used whenever his name came up. Later that night, he mentioned it to his wife, hoping she could provide some insight.

"The women all say that I am an 'unk,'" Roger said with obvious concern. "What does this mean?"

Kathleen looked at him strangely, not at all sure. "I don't know. Maybe it's short for *uncle.* . . ."

"They were all in the dining room, and I heard them say that I am such an *unk.* It seemed like a good thing, but I wasn't sure."

Her face lit up and she laughed. "They're saying you're a *hunk.* You didn't pronounce the *H,* so I didn't understand at first. Yes, Roger, it's a very good thing. It means they think you're an attractive man."

Even in his late sixties, Roger possessed a European elegance and mystique that most women find compelling. I thought he looked like a French Robert De Niro. (I once even asked him to do the signature grimace De Niro is famous for, and it confirmed my belief.) But that was all much later, long after he nearly drenched me with dirty water, which seemed almost appropriate, given my mood.

"No worries," I said after I'd hopped back a foot to avoid the spray. "I probably shouldn't be standing here looking like my dog just got run over."

Roger looked a bit confused. "I'm sure that is a metaphor, which doesn't feel very positive. I wish I could change it with a full breakfast, but it's not ready yet. There is coffee, though, if that helps bring your dog back."

His joke made me smile, which was exactly what I needed to break the spell. *It wasn't as if I had been with Michele for that long,* I thought to myself. We had only gotten together twice before, after meeting at a conference in Toronto, and we had decided to spend a week together to *explore* where we wanted things to go. After a day and a half we came to Drew House, which a friend had recommended. And that's when everything seemed to shift. I began feeling a strange gap growing between us, and it didn't take long for it to become as big as the famous gorge a half mile up the road.

"Coffee sounds great," I said as I followed Roger through the door.

We walked into the small kitchen, which seemed both modern and ancient at the same time. Bins of produce were stacked next to the door, and stainless-steel equipment stood beside old-school appliances, like the dishwasher in the corner that reminded me of the one I used in my first job when I was sixteen. I immediately had the sense that this was a kitchen that belonged to someone who knew what he was doing, a professional who had dedicated his life to the art of food. On the other hand, the small size and compact nature made it feel less like a commercial enterprise and more like a tiny oasis. Roger picked up a French press and scooped three large spoonfuls of coffee into it, then poured in hot water from a teakettle.

"When you are at home," he said over his shoulder, "how do you make your coffee? Do you have an espresso machine?"

"I used to, but now I use a little automatic drip that makes one cup at a time. I do have a French press as well, though."

"It's better to use one of these," he said as he stirred the coffee grounds and water.

"Look at what happens as I stir—it creates this foam at the top, just like espresso. It also doesn't oxidize the coffee like a drip machine, especially if you leave it on the burner too long. Any more than a few minutes and it starts to go bad . . . and it doesn't only taste bitter, but it's not very good for you. It takes all the joy out of drinking a great cup of coffee, which is why we do it. Whatever brings us joy, we do; and what makes us feel sick, we don't."

"Is that your philosophy for life? Do what brings you joy or makes you feel good?"

"Of course," Roger remarked with a sweeping gesture of his hand, then motioned for me to sit down on a stool in the corner. "This is why we're here on the planet . . . but not just to make *ourselves* feel good. The best life is the one that brings joy to others—that is the way to happiness. This is why I love to cook, because when I use the best ingredients I can find and put love into everything I make, it changes people's moods . . . and sometimes even their lives.

"Most have no idea that there's such a strong relationship between the intention of the chef and the quality of the meal. You can take two new cooks who are just beginning to learn, and they use the exact same recipe and all the same ingredients, but when everything is finished, one is absolutely amazing and the other is so-so. Why? Because the first cook put his heart into every step: cutting the vegetables, stirring the pot, cooking the sauce. The other was following a recipe—too much in his head, not in his heart."

I noticed a large skillet on the gas stove with some oil simmering at the bottom, then the small pile of diced white potatoes and yams on the cutting board. Roger used a knife to scoop up the potatoes and place them into the pan. With the agility of a master, he tossed and mixed the contents together and then set the pan onto a burner and lowered the flame.

"These need to cook slowly; otherwise, they'll burn and lose their flavor." He then turned around and walked to the other side of the kitchen, reaching his hand into a bag and producing a large bunch of garlic. "I buy these at a market not too far from here. They're locally grown and cost about four times more than what I would pay at the grocery store, but it's worth it to have such wonderful, fresh ingredients."

"So the whole thing you were saying about focusing on making others happy," I said, wanting to return to the previous discussion.

"What about someone who just doesn't want it? I mean . . . those who can't let themselves feel joy, no matter what happens."

"Are you speaking about yourself or that lovely woman you came in here with?" he asked with a smile.

"I guess it could be either of us," I responded, a bit embarrassed. "She just abandoned me because she thinks we're too different. I just wanted to get to know her better and maybe move a step closer to a relationship. . . ."

"A step closer?" Roger was still smiling. "Love usually doesn't go in neat steps—it's rarely so well organized. Maybe that's the problem: you want it to go a certain way and can't see the real direction it's moving on its own. We want nice, clean steps because we want to control our emotions, usually because we're afraid of being out of control. Take this garlic, for example." He picked up a large cutting knife and separated a single clove from the bunch.

"Most people say it's best to cut the garlic in little slivers—they think it brings out the flavor. What they don't realize is that garlic has a very interesting quality: it heals itself after it's been cut, just like your finger would. Your finger wants to retain your blood; the garlic wants to retain its juice. You chop the garlic slowly, carefully, and by the time you put it on the fire, it's locked its juice inside. Let me show you a better way to do it."

He separated two more cloves and smashed the flat end of the knife down with great force, destroying them both. "Now it can't heal itself, and look . . . the juice is completely exposed and can really be tasted."

He could tell by my look that I couldn't see the connection between my experience with Michele and the proper way to prepare garlic.

"What I'm saying," he continued, "is that your life is not meant to be slowly dissected . . . it is meant to be smashed. Then the juice inside you flows out and adds flavor to everything you touch. When you try to control the circumstances and the people around you, you're doing so out of fear. Don't give too much or you might be left with too little—that kind of thing. You stop the flow of life as soon as it starts. So you need to let go of the fear and let it spill out into the world like this garlic."

Roger used the knife to pick up the smashed bits as well as the juice and deposited it into the pan with the potatoes. A plume of steam rose when it hit the hot oil, and he lifted the pan and stirred it without the benefit of a utensil, tossing its contents into the air in a flurry of color and fragrant aroma.

"Most people try to live an overly sanitized life," he continued, "as if being clean and being pure are the same thing." He reached behind him and produced a bowl filled with discolored salt.

"This is sea salt. It isn't pure white like the salt you probably use. It's a bit brown and has little bits of earth mixed in it. It's so much better for you than anything else because the so-called impurities are what make it healthy." He withdrew two pinches of salt and spread it evenly into the mix of potatoes and garlic.

"These are the things that make a great breakfast because they aren't perfect. The salt has some color to it, the garlic has been smashed so the juice flows, and the vegetables haven't been cut with precision by a machine. And then there's the love that blends it all together, making the most delicious hash browns. If we could live our lives in the same way, then most of our problems would vanish in an instant."

"How did you learn to cook like this?" I asked him.

"Growing up in France, my mother always taught me to practice simplicity and handle everything with love. That's the secret, not only to French cooking, but to everything in life. Simple, high-quality ingredients . . . if you start with that, then the rest is easy. I don't really consider myself a great chef. I just know how to shop."

"How to shop?"

"When I was young, I learned to go to the farms and to the local places to buy the best produce and meats. Even now when I visit a new city, I always have a feeling about where the boats come in, and I buy right from the ocean. I can almost smell it in the air, which always surprises my wife. When it's something you've been raised with, it comes naturally. So that's my formula: start with the best, natural ingredients, and always cook with love."

I was impressed by the life Roger had created for himself in Elora. I later learned that he had owned one of the most successful restaurants in Toronto, then sold it and moved to Australia for a kind of sabbatical, but food was too much in his blood to stop. He opened a French pastry shop, and before long it was the hit of the town. Sixteen years later, he returned to Canada and started running the bed-and-breakfast with Kathleen. She had been renting a room at Drew House when he was in Australia, but when he returned, the friendship developed into a budding romance. The business they created together seemed in perfect balance with who they were as people and as a couple. It was impressive to experience firsthand.

"I think you may have found the secret of abundance as well as cooking," I told him. "When I look around, everything seems so well balanced. Do you consider yourself to be abundant?"

"Let me tell you a story about someone who is extremely abundant," Roger replied. "A few years ago, a local gentleman who had done really well for himself wanted to put together a dinner for charity and flew in Alain Dutournier from Paris to prepare the meal. Alain is one of the greatest chefs around—a real superstar. The organizers of the event decided to have him stay with us at Drew House—I guess because they figured he would feel more at home. He had no idea when he came that it was owned by another Frenchman, and the entire time he was here I insisted that he relax and allow me to cook for him.

"This was a man who spent all his time cooking for others, creating spectacular dishes that won international awards. At night we would drink wine together and compare stories. Well, one evening I asked him a question: if he had only one night left on Earth, what would his last meal be? I expected haute cuisine—he's such a talented chef—but he went in a completely different direction. He told me that he'd make himself fried eggs."

"You're kidding! Why would he choose eggs if he could have anything he wanted?"

"Think about it for a moment. You're right—this is a man who could have anything, the very finest in the world. But what he connected with more was a feeling. He shared that when he was young, his mother would make him eggs every morning. But for his last meal, he didn't just want ordinary eggs. They would have to be fried in duck or goose fat because it's the very best. He would collect the eggs from the chicken coop behind his house. He would also go out into the garden and pick a single green pepper, and buy some fresh bread from the baker down the street. This is what his final meal would consist of—a powerful reminder of the love his mother gave him through the food she served. To Alain, this was the best meal he could have; and to me, this is what true abundance is."

"You're saying that abundance has less to do with what you have than what you feel?"

"Exactly. Most people think it's about how much money you make or how big your house is. Alain has all that, but he knows it's not what's important. Love is what is important, and the feeling he gets when he's tuned in to that energy. His mother was a symbol of something inside him. She was probably the first person who made him feel whole and connected with something bigger than himself. When I asked him that question, he went back to that time in his mind, and to the food she served him. It was simple, which is why he wanted it more than anything else."

I thought about my own life and all the time I'd spent searching for money and fame. Achieving those things meant that I was worthy and deserving of love; without them, I believed I didn't have anything to offer another person. When I was younger, before I had attained any sort of financial or professional success, I didn't think I was capable of attracting lasting love. I was never powerful enough or rich enough, no matter what the circumstances were. It dawned on me that in forty-eight years, I hadn't experienced a relationship that lasted more than a few years. I'd been successful and had earned more money than I thought possible, but I didn't feel abundant.

"How about you?" I asked Roger. "It seems like you've lived a good life. Do you consider yourself a success?"

"I remember when I owned my restaurant in downtown Toronto. It was a big success, and people came from all over to eat there. Of course, I made lots of money and became pretty well known. Now I'm far away from the city and the prestige, and I'm happier than I've ever been. As far as money goes, I make much less today, but I feel rich. That's because I love what I'm doing. I have a wonderful wife, and I get to cook delicious food for people, even if it's just breakfast. For me, it isn't about how much—it's about the quality of my life."

As Roger spoke, he took out another pan, poured olive oil into it, and lit another burner. He reached over to a bowl that contained six or so eggs, and after waiting for the oil to heat, he gently broke them one at a time into the pan.

"If I had goose or duck fat I would use it now, but olive oil will have to do."

"I'm amazed at how spiritual cooking is for you," I said to him. "I almost feel like I'm in church, listening to a sermon on the best way to live a holy life."

"Food is one of the closest things we have to *real* spirituality," Roger replied. "Why do you think so much attention is given to the Last Supper? In my opinion, most people miss the point of it altogether. For example, Catholics get caught up in the idea that it really is the body and blood of Jesus, and they miss its greatest message. Jesus was trying to teach his disciples a very simple lesson. He looked around the table where they were sitting and picked up the two most ordinary things he could find: bread and wine. They were always there, so much so that people would take them for granted, and this is why he chose those things for one of the most important lessons he ever taught.

"Jesus said, 'This is my body,' because he wanted us to see the divinity in something as ordinary as bread and to be mindful every time we consumed it. Then he said, 'This is my blood,' because he wanted us to see the correlation between something we have every day and the sacredness that's always around us. The message was that the energy of love is ever present and can be found in the simplest elements."

"I thought everyone from France was Catholic," I said to him, half joking. "Did you ever see it as being Jesus's body and blood?"

"I see it exactly in that way, but not to the exclusion of anything else. I see the eggs in that way, and the garlic, too. Did you know that in the earliest paintings depicting the Last Supper, there is hardly anything on the table? As our lives became more complex, filled with more 'things,' the foods placed before Jesus and his disciples evolved into a feast. That's what we usually do—complicate the very simple teachings of Jesus so we don't have to really understand them. We're more comfortable if it's abstract or hidden in symbolism instead of being right in front of us, even on our kitchen table."

"But you do believe that the Last Supper actually occurred, right?"

"I *know* that it really happened," he said with more conviction than I expected. "I can feel it deep inside myself, but not necessarily in the way most people think. It was a celebration of Jesus's life because he was the only one who knew it was his final meal. He knew what was about to happen, and rather than be alone, he wanted to be with the people he loved. He washed their feet when they first came into the room—this was unusual and even unheard of at the time. Then he had everyone sit down, and he fed them physically and spiritually. I sometimes wonder if the apostles realized what he was giving them: an example of how they needed to treat one another."

"You said that the food was both physical *and* spiritual. Does that mean we should see every meal we eat in the same way?"

"Well, all meals are physical, obviously," Roger noted. "But they are also spiritual. It depends upon the spirit in which we receive the food we eat. If we're grateful for the entire lineage—meaning, the farmer, the baker, or the animal or plant itself—then it nourishes our soul.

"I think that's something the French have always understood. We don't rush through a good meal like people do here. We take our time, relishing every aspect, including appreciating those who are at the table with us. That is what feeds us spiritually. To me, *that* is what religion truly is."

I took a long sip from the cup of coffee Roger had poured for me. In that moment, I thought it was the best coffee I had ever tasted, and for the first time I considered the possibility that I hadn't come to Drew House for Michele or for any other obvious reason. Maybe I was there to learn something deeper—something that could only be appreciated through food and the tutelage of a master chef, as well as a master of life. I sat back on the stool and took a deep breath.

"I really have a lot to learn, don't I?"

CHAPTER TWO

Your Life Is Meant to Be Smashed

Food is one of the closest things we have to real spirituality. The phrase swam through my head for the rest of the afternoon, especially as I tried to figure out what I was going to do next. I was scheduled to fly back to Oregon in three days, but since Michele had left, I needed to make a decision. Should I catch an earlier flight back to Portland? I could get a ride into Toronto and do who knows what, but the idea of wandering around the city by myself left me feeling hollow.

The more I pondered, the more I realized that I wanted to stay at Drew House and listen to the guy with the thick accent talk about love, God, and the art of French cooking. Roger's words were breaking through my consciousness in ways I had never really experienced . . . so maybe I *should* stick around and see what I could learn.

I crossed Mill Street and walked down to the river to sit alone for a while. I needed some self-reflection, considering everything that had already happened that day. The experience with Michele was just another in a long list of romantic miscalculations, and I was growing more and more accustomed to being left before I was even *in* a relationship. I couldn't seem to put my finger on what I'd done to set Michele off, or for that matter, the three or four women before her. As I sat down on a bench overlooking the spot where the water plunged several feet into the awaiting swell, I silently acknowledged that I didn't want to know. I was blocking something, and although I had come far enough to pinpoint this fact, I was still no closer to figuring out what it was I didn't want to see.

I looked to the other side of the river and took in the thirty-foot cliff with the expensive homes perched over the falls. Several trees in the area seemed to hang in a delicate balancing act, gripping the thin soil that kept them attached to the cliff's edge. Some of the trees were tall and straight, as if they had found a way to angle their roots deeper in the direction of the earth, while others had lost the battle and were hanging upside down, clinging to their lives in a desperate war of opposing wills.

The open sky seemed to beckon the trees toward heaven while gravity pulled them back toward the earth, as if afraid to let them fly. Clumps of grass and entwined roots were the only things that prevented them from plunging into the cold water below. Their fall was inevitable, of course, just as death and decay are . . . just as it was inevitable for me to find myself upside down once again.

I returned to Drew House and walked up the stairs to my room. Now that I was on my own, I could sleep on whichever side of the bed I wanted, but it was small consolation considering that I would have preferred to be next to Michele. My thoughts returned to wondering what I had said or done to make her unwilling to even give me a ride back to the airport in Toronto. I started to replay the previous night in my mind, hoping to identify the key moment when things had apparently gone awry.

"I'm not sure why you even want to be here with me," Michele said as we finished our dinner at the restaurant. The place was nearly deserted, and I was pouring cream into my coffee while Michele stared blankly at the cup of tea in front of her.

"What do you mean?" I asked. "I want to be with you because I like you. Isn't that enough?"

"It *would* be enough if it were true," she replied. "I thought it was when we first met. God, you went completely overboard making sure I knew how you felt. Now it's different, but I can't explain why."

"How am I supposed to know what to do if you can't tell me how I'm being different? I don't think anything has changed. I flew here to see you, and we're staying at this great B&B eating at a little restaurant in a town I'd never heard of before. I'm not claiming to know where things are going with us or how long we'll be together, but we're together right now. That's all that matters to me."

"This is what I'm saying." Her dramatic tone didn't seem to fit her words. "I'm not asking you to know anything or tell me what the next five years are going to look like. But I would like to feel that you're really here with me, not off somewhere in your mind more focused on where you'll be next week."

I could feel my insides beginning to tighten up and retreat into the safe cave within, a room no one could enter but me. It was the only place I felt secure—where no one could reach me. On the walls of the cave I could see pictures from my youth: baseball cards and rock posters, many of which had been part of the original decor when I had first established this safe haven. Interspersed between the 1970s memorabilia were more modern elements that had been added over time—first from my college years, then from my marriage, which had ended many years before. It was more of a bunker than a room, with windowless walls and thick impenetrable ramparts.

Michele was beginning to push, and even though I didn't want to run away from her, I felt myself being pulled into the darkness where I felt calm and at ease.

The conversation progressed in that direction until we were back at Drew House getting ready for bed. There was a moment when I thought I had successfully lightened the mood, but it was quickly dampened. More than anything, this told me that we really were in trouble. The fact that my charm and sense of humor were no match for the heaviness that now enveloped us made me feel like I was drowning. I felt an almost overwhelming sinking sensation.

Michele wouldn't even change out of her clothes that night, as if she were waiting for the sun to rise so she could escape. And that's exactly what she did. When morning came, she quietly packed her bag and turned toward me before walking out the door.

"I wish I could blame you for this, but I can't. We just see things from very different angles. It's not that I'm right and you're wrong—it's just that you were born one way and I was born another. I don't think you can change that."

"You know, when I was younger, I considered myself a Republican," I replied, hoping to say something that might make her want to stay. "I remember my brother backing McGovern in the '72 election, and even though I was only ten, I was for Nixon. Of course, I didn't know what I was talking about—I was just mouthing my father's words. I was probably the same way all through high school, but in college I began to change. It wasn't something I was born with—I've just always been able to look at things in a new way and make a different decision. That makes it hard for me to believe what you're saying . . . that we're born into a locked position that remains constant our entire lives. It feels like you're saying we're all victims."

"I'm *not* a victim," she answered under her breath, and it was the last thing she said before picking up her bag and walking out the door. I followed her down to the parking lot and for the first time thought it might be better that things simply end. She got into the car and drove away, leaving my liberal ass without a ride.

As I was lying on the bed, looking up at the ceiling, I started wondering if it was a good idea to remain at Drew House. Maybe I should take a taxi back to Toronto and get on the next flight to Portland. Part of me wanted to run away, something I was very good at, while another voice seemed to be calling me in a different direction. It wanted me to stay and spend more time with the enigmatic chef who seemed to know so much about love and life.

I had the feeling that Roger had the answer I had been searching for, although I wasn't exactly sure what the question was. The only thing I was certain about was that one door had closed, and just as quickly, another had opened . . . but I couldn't decide if I wanted to step through it.

I got up and thought I'd explore the house to give myself something to do. The dining room was dark, and there was no sound coming from the kitchen. Looking at the pictures and decorations that filled the room, it was easy to feel the European influence. I noticed two large paintings of men playing a game with a long basket attached to their hands. They were dressed in white clothing, which seemed unsuited for playing such an active sport. One player appeared to be running toward a goal, but that was all I could decipher. I was staring at the pictures when I heard a noise behind me, then turned to see Roger walking toward me wearing a light jacket.

"That's a sport called *chistera*," he said. "It's played where I come from in the Basque area of France. It's very popular—well, at least it used to be."

"Did you ever play it yourself?" I asked him.

"Oh yes, but not seriously. We say that it's the fastest game in the world. Really good players can throw the rubber ball over three hundred kilometers an hour with one of those gloves on. It can be very dangerous if you get hit."

"I was just walking around and thought I'd see if you needed help with anything," I said, hoping he didn't mind me following after him like a puppy.

"Well, I was going to stop by a farmers' market to buy some produce and then visit one of my favorite spots in the forest to go mushrooming. You're welcome to join me if you want to."

I said I did and walked out with Roger to his truck. We pulled onto the street and headed into Elora, then turned left and crossed the bridge that led back to the highway.

"I'd love to hear more about your life growing up in France," I said to him. "You mentioned earlier that your mother greatly influenced your cooking technique, right?"

"Yes. I mostly learned from my grandmother and mother—also my aunt. They taught me the most important things, most of which I still practice today, especially how to look for a certain life force in everything I work with. If something is alive, it has an energy that enhances life; if it's dead—like most processed foods we see today—then it has very little benefit and can even be harmful. If you stick with that one practice—buying what is alive—then everything you make will be great, even if you aren't the most skilled cook."

"Is your mother still alive?"

"No, she's been gone for a long time now." Roger looked pensive. "Right after she was born, she was sold to a Basque family who raised her. Her birth mother was a young beauty who fell in love with a Polish soldier. When she became pregnant, her parents didn't want her to shame the family, so they arranged to have the baby sold to people who lived a good distance away. When my mother was growing up, she stood out because she had blonde hair, which was never seen in Basque Country."

"What was she like?"

"Put it this way," he said, smiling. "If there's an adventurous bone in my body, it came from her. She was even part of the Resistance during the war. She would smuggle messages and help people escape the Nazis. You can imagine how dangerous that was, and many of her friends were killed. In fact, my uncle was killed just a few days before the war ended."

We were driving through the countryside past farms and empty fields. Roger explained that the area was predominantly Mennonite, and most of the families who farmed the land possessed few of the luxuries we often take for granted. Ancient-looking barns reminded me of rural parts in Pennsylvania where the Amish community thrives. I remembered driving through the area as a child with my father when we ran out of gas. The fact that we were in a place where the average family didn't own a car made the dilemma more memorable. We were lucky to find a farmer who had a half-filled gas can on reserve for a generator he'd never actually used. We raced away as fast as possible, hoping to get back to "civilization" before we got stuck again.

"There are two or three farm stands I usually stop at," Roger told me. "The owners understand me and let me do my thing."

"What do you mean?" I had the feeling that *doing his thing* would be interesting to watch.

"I was taught to let the produce talk to me," he said, then gave me a wink, which made me wonder if he was pulling my leg. "Anything will talk to you if you listen in the right way. When I pick up a squash or an onion, I feel it with my fingers and let it speak to my soul. If it's ready and wants to be in my pot, then it tells me."

"You're joking now, right?"

"Maybe a little. It *is* true that food speaks to us, but most people are too literal with this kind of thing. We need to listen with our feelings, not just our ears. I've been doing this for so many years that I get a sense of when something is right and when it isn't. Most of all, I've learned to trust the feeling, which is something most people aren't able to do."

"Trust themselves?"

"Yes," Roger explained. "It's a skill we learn and develop through practice. That's also something I learned when I was younger. There's an intuitive language that every living thing understands . . . whether it's a human being, a dog, or a plant. Sometimes we just know something, although we don't know how we came to know it.

"Someone may tell you that you're wrong or that your words are nonsense, but if it's inside you, then you're able to see past everything and prove it for yourself. This is how I treat food, as well as everything else in my life. When I'm cooking, I feel as if I'm communicating with all the ingredients, and that's why I don't usually measure things or follow recipes too closely. After so many years, I've developed the skill of just *knowing,* and I find that the more I trust myself, the better the meal turns out."

"That's something I could use some practice with," I remarked. "One of my problems is that I tend to go against what I know, and it never turns out well in the end. I think that's what happened with Michele. Even when things were looking really good between us, I knew deep down that it wasn't going to turn out like it was in my imagination. I had this fantasy that she was perfect for me and that we were going to get married eventually. At the same time, there was this other voice telling me to let it go . . . but I didn't want to listen."

"Maybe the real message was to stop looking for perfection in someone else, and to realize that *you* are perfect."

"That sounds like something I heard in a movie."

"Maybe you have," Roger continued. "Nothing is ever original —that is, no one is ever going to play that role until you play it for yourself. *Perfect* doesn't mean that there are no flaws; it means that in spite of the flaws, you're willing to love. Even when things don't appear the way you want them to, you keep your heart open. Then you're able to see that everything is perfect just the way it is—especially you. I guarantee you'll never see the perfection in another person until you see it in yourself."

We pulled up to a small produce stand, and Roger turned off the engine. I had the sudden sensation that we were entering a different world, one where plants and vegetables spoke in hushed voices to anyone willing to listen. Roger waved to an elderly woman sitting in the corner of the tent, and she smiled back in recognition.

"Hello, my friend," she said in a happy voice. "I was wondering when you would come by."

"This is my friend James," Roger said as we walked through the rows of fruits and vegetables. "He's staying with us and spending the day teaching me about love."

"I'm teaching *you*?" I asked, surprised.

"I have the feeling that you're the teacher," the woman answered, pointing to Roger. "You strike me as one who knows more than he lets on."

"The only thing I know is what I'm able to see," he said, "and when I'm with James, I see the part of me that understands a little, but still has a lot to learn. That's why he's my teacher today."

I stared at Roger, wondering what to think of the comment. I wasn't sure if he was giving me a compliment or a clever challenge. Before I had the chance to reply, he was already moving from bin to bin picking up carrots and onions, smelling them, and as far as I could tell, listening to what they had to say. If not for the conversation we'd had in the car, I wouldn't have paid much attention to what he was doing, but now I had a very different attitude. If there really was a method to his madness, I wanted to understand it.

We visited two other stands, and the experience was very similar to the first. Everyone gave Roger a warm welcome; he was clearly someone they respected and enjoyed. I was also noticing something else, something less obvious, and I wondered if the others picked up on it, too.

I was beginning to think that Roger was a rare spiritual teacher who used food as inspiration for his lessons. There seemed to be something behind everything he said, as if the whole world would open up if I paid close attention. He was hidden in a way, veiled behind the meals he prepared and the simple lessons that flowed from him so effortlessly. I could have just as easily been in a Buddhist temple or monastery than a bed-and-breakfast an hour outside Toronto, keeping company with a man who was proving to be more of a sage with every word he spoke.

"How many restaurants have you owned?" I asked as we were leaving the Mennonite country and heading toward Roger's favorite mushrooming spot.

"I had my first restaurant in France when I was very young. I put everything I had into it—all my money and a little bit that I got from my parents. Of course, I wanted to make a good living, but I never really thought about the money. My passion was the most important thing to me, and I think people responded to it. I didn't have many dishes when I first opened . . . maybe five or six. But I did every one of them very well. My specialty was fish soup. People came from all over to have it, and to this day it's probably my best dish. I always figured that it's better to do a few dishes extremely well than to have a big menu and only be okay.

"I also owned a few restaurants when I moved to Toronto in the early '60s," Roger added. "It was very hard getting started, but once we were rolling, it was a great success. I remember that my accountant always had a problem with how much I spent on ingredients. My food costs were somewhere around 44 percent, which was much higher than anywhere else. If you think of a low place, like a fast-food restaurant, the food cost is about 17 percent or less; while most good restaurants would be around 28 percent.

"So there I was with incredible expenses, but my tables were always full. My accountant came in and said, 'Roger, your costs are way too high! You have to cut down because you don't make enough money.' Well, I looked at him and said, 'Martin, I never made so much money in my whole life.' He tells me I could be making more—probably double. I said, 'I don't give a shit about your figures of how much I should or shouldn't be making. My customers are happy and they keep coming back. And I'm happy, so why should I cheat these people out of what I give them?' Martin accepted this because he saw that I did make money year after year. He promised to never tell me what to do again."

"Raising prices might have driven people away, and you wouldn't have been nearly as successful," I pointed out.

"Exactly. That is why the logic of accountants is not necessarily the logic of God, who says that we must give everything to everything. Do you know what I mean by that?"

"I think I do. It means not to hold back; give more than just your money—give your energy and passion as often as you can."

Roger nodded. "God doesn't keep lists of percentages and figures. He cares about our essence and, of course, sharing that essence. Jesus talked about the woman who gave a few pennies and that her gift was so much greater than the man who gave a large sum. Why? Because it was all the money she had, and it was a sacrifice to give it away. The rich man may have given more, but it didn't cost him anything. He didn't *feel* it in the same way.

"The woman gave her essence because she believed that it would return to her. This is also why Jesus challenged his disciples to sell what they had and give the money to the poor. I don't know if he really meant that we have to be poor ourselves; it was more of a spiritual lesson about the importance of giving all the time.

"That's the beauty of food as well. Do you think an apple or a carrot holds back when it offers itself to us to eat? They give their essence because they know that it will then live within us. When we give our essence to another, it continues on through the life of another. That is the logic of God."

Minutes later Roger parked the car alongside a busy highway and took two baskets out of the back. He motioned for me to follow him down a path that led into a thick forest. The sounds of the road soon disappeared as we were enveloped by another world.

"This is the best area I've found for finding mushrooms," Roger declared. "It might be a bit early for them, but it's worth a try. It's a real gift when they're here, and I love to share them with my friends. I only keep as many as I need for the dishes I'm going to make for the next few days."

"I've never done this before," I said to him. "Is there anything I need to know?"

"For me, this is a sacred experience. It's being connected to the earth . . . a very good way to let go of all the things that don't matter, and focus on what is simple and right in front of you. It's difficult to spot the mushrooms—you must give it your full attention, especially right now when they're not so plentiful. If you are present and let your gaze move along the surface, then you might find an area that's rich with growth. Either way, even if neither of us finds any, it's a great spiritual practice."

I followed him off the path and watched as he picked up a branch from the ground and used it to brush aside leaves and other small branches. I did the same, and before long I realized that I was moving in a different direction, into a shallow ravine where the foliage was growing more and more dense. It was as if I didn't have a choice about where I was going. Something seemed to be pulling me farther from Roger and deeper into the forest, and I hoped it would lead to some success. After a few minutes, I hadn't seen a single mushroom, and I thought that he was right about it being too early. Then again, I had the sense that I was there for something more, so I continued with my eyes on the ground, searching for a colony of fungi.

I suddenly flashed on a time when I was around fourteen, hiking aimlessly through the woods near my family's home. The memory was so vivid that everything else seemed to fade, including my adult form; I was a kid again, thinking and wondering about the same issues that seemed so important to me at the time. I had just graduated from eighth grade and was nervous about going to high school. Most of my friends would be attending a different public school while I was to enter the Catholic school on the other side of town. That meant new friends, a new environment, and new pressure that I had to face. I was overwhelmed by the fear building inside of me.

The fear was so strong that I didn't think I was going to make it. I felt an urge to keep on walking so I could disappear, never to be seen again. I could learn to live off the land and forage for survival. I even thought that if I needed to, I could sneak into town every night and steal from the people who lived at the edge of the forest. They would never know I was there, and I could go on living a life that seemed far more attractive than what I was about to encounter. The notion of facing the fear hiding within me was far too scary and risky, and even though I knew I was daydreaming, escaping seemed to be a much more viable option.

As quickly as I left, I was back in the real world, no longer fourteen, but forty-eight. I wanted to hold on to the powerful emotions and try to understand why I was so terrified at the time—what I couldn't face then but might be able to now. I decided to let the memory wash over me again, hoping that a feeling might rise out of the darkness, revealing the shadowy figure that had been chasing me for so long.

I took a deep breath, never letting my eyes leave the dirt and vines that covered the ground. They were like hypnotic triggers that pulled me back to a former life, one that seemed far more distant than it really was. Then without warning, something seemed to be forming. I held my breath as I recognized the features of my younger self. I heard a whisper at first, but then it began to build in intensity, rushing through me and my younger self at the same time: *You don't deserve to be happy.*

There was no reason or purpose for why that emerged, only the familiar sensation of unworthiness and the sense that I'd never be capable of experiencing lasting love or peace. I buried the feeling then, and it had remained buried in my unconscious mind for decades. Now it was here again, a ghost from the past, and I didn't know what to do.

I fell to one knee and started gasping for air. Thoughts of Roger filled my mind, and I hoped he was far away from this spot, unable to witness this assault. My fourteen-year-old self was the more dominant one now, and as much as I tried to force him out of my mind, he wouldn't leave. There had to be a reason for feeling this again—for letting the fear emerge and testing its strength. Perhaps that was the real purpose, I considered—to gauge the truth of a feeling I couldn't understand at the time and see if it was anything more than a phantom that had been hiding inside me.

Its influence certainly felt concrete and real. I began to see that this fear had been controlling the movement of my entire life in ways I'd never realized—ways that I was unable to perceive until this very moment. I'd carried it for so long that it was a normal part of me, and that, I suddenly knew, was the source of its power. The fear had merged with my consciousness so well that I viewed it as a natural part of me, a friend—albeit, one that was veiled and disturbed.

I tried to shake it free, but it wouldn't budge. Too much time had been invested; too many years had passed to allow it to be so easily forsaken. Then I realized that pushing it away wasn't what I needed. There was another possibility now that the feeling had surfaced, for as much as I wanted to deny it, it was still a part of me. As wrong as it was in its assessment of who I was and what I deserved, it had been the most consistent friend I had ever known. It wasn't something to cast out, but to embrace.

Then it dawned on me: I was finally ready to see it for what it really was—an ancient belief that no longer had any relevance. But like an old friend I no longer had much in common with, it didn't need to be cut out of my life. A new relationship needed to emerge, one where it was validated but given limited attention.

A peaceful sensation washed through me, and I felt the strength return to my limbs. I didn't know how that new relationship would happen or if the feeling would ever show itself again, but I had achieved something significant. I was victorious. I took a deep breath of fresh air, hoping I was right.

I stood up and brushed off my pants. The basket, still empty, was sitting at my feet, and I picked it up and started walking. Seconds later, I heard Roger's voice calling me, and I followed it until I saw the path. It led me out of the woods and into the light, somewhere I felt destined to live.

CHAPTER
THREE

Love Lies Bleeding

The next morning I woke up and reached behind me to touch Michele. It took about three seconds to remember that she wasn't there and that I was still alone. I closed my eyes and held perfectly still for several minutes, hoping I would fall back into whatever dream I'd inhabited before being struck by that sad realization. I recalled yesterday's walk through the forest hunting for mushrooms and the overwhelming sensation of missing out on the life I had once been promised. *Where had it all gone?*

I couldn't blame thirty years of wandering on a lonely fourteen-year-old who was afraid of starting a new school. It was too simple and easily dismissed. There was something else—something that was much more current and daunting that was hidden from my attention. As I was lying in bed, I realized that whatever it was, it was the key to everything I was feeling: all the ways I'd been pushing away happiness and love, and why I wasn't able to relax into the life I had chosen for myself.

Facing the new day also meant confronting the real reason I was alone and why I wouldn't allow any woman to get too close. I pulled the blanket over my shoulders and tried to relax my mind, breathing deeply to entice sleep. It didn't come, and the longer I lay there, the deeper I plunged into loneliness. I finally stood up and walked to the sink, hoping the shock of cool water splashed on my face would break the cheerless atmosphere.

I eventually walked down to the kitchen where I knew Roger would be. The thought of once again sitting on the stool and listening to his discourse on life and love lifted my mood considerably. A couple was seated in the dining room as another was getting up to leave. An older woman was eating fruit salad while her husband stirred his coffee. They were just starting to eat their breakfast. I glanced over to the kitchen and saw Roger moving about, standing over the stove one second, then disappearing deeper into the room the next. I wasn't sure if I was welcome to join him, but after a few seconds, I decided to try my luck. Peeking around the open door, I caught his attention, and a wide smile lit up his face.

"Bonjour," he said as he pulled out the stool for me. "I had a feeling you would be down soon. Here, have a seat while I prepare breakfast for the couple in the dining room."

I sat down, and within seconds, Roger was pouring me a cup of coffee. I added cream and sugar, which were sitting on the cutting board next to me.

"You know, I woke up this morning with an interesting line in my head," Roger said. "It was: *Everything is simple once you know how to do it*. What do you think that means?"

"That has to be one of the most obvious statements I've ever heard," I replied as I took a sip of coffee.

Roger nodded and continued. "And yet it's something that escapes most people. We tend to overcomplicate things instead of doing simple things very, very well. In terms of cooking, the secret is quality and not doing too much."

"Too much?" I asked. "How can something become simple unless you do it enough times so it becomes easy or second nature?"

"I mean not trying to impress others or not trying to be something other than what you are deep down in your heart. The master is one who does what is simple, but in a way that seems remarkable. Do you understand what I mean by that?"

"It means to . . . well—"

"To be a master of anything, you have to honor the source. For example, if you're a spiritual master, then you always begin by honoring the source of life, or God. If you are a master painter, then you honor the other masters who inspired you. If you are a master chef, then you honor the source of the food you prepare—the earth, the soil, the water, and every natural thing that brought the food into your kitchen. This is not something they teach you in cooking school. Chefs are usually taught to respect themselves and their skills rather than those who make their work possible.

"So this is something I try to never forget. I always think about the farmer or the fisherman or whoever else worked to bring this food into my kitchen. If I can keep my focus and energy there, then it flows into whatever I'm making. People can taste the love . . . not just from me, but from everyone else who helped me."

Roger spoke as he grated several potatoes, forming a pile on the cutting board in front of him. Once he had a large quantity, he picked up a handful and squeezed the juice out into the sink.

"I'm making Rösti potatoes," he said as he worked. "It's a Swiss recipe made popular by the farmers in the area around Bern. Many people consider it to be their national dish, and it's remarkably simple to make. It's basically potato pancakes, but it sounds much nicer when you call them by the German name."

"Do you usually serve them to your guests here?" I asked, not really sure what to say, but wanting to keep the conversation moving.

"Not too often, but I wanted to make them for you because of everything we've been talking about. Once again, the best things are often the most simple. People think that French cooking is so complicated and difficult to learn. It can be if they do it the way it's usually taught, but for me, it's more important for it to be accessible and easy to imitate. You've never cooked in your life . . . is that true?"

"Is it that obvious?" I asked.

"Well, yes and no. I can't tell from anything you've said or asked—just by the way you've been watching me. It's like a child watching his mother or father, wanting to absorb everything his parent is doing so he can imitate it later. I can tell by the way you move your eyes that this is all new to you."

"It's true. I've never really learned to cook. I can't tell you how much money I've spent going to restaurants instead of eating at home."

"Well, this is something you'll be able to make," Roger replied, smiling. "And it may very well impress someone you make it for.

Once you squeeze all the juice out of the potatoes, take two eggs and a little bit of salt, and mix them all together. The eggs will help bind the ingredients when it comes time for cooking."

Roger moved his hands through the mixture with expert control and formed several small pancakes, placing them onto a hot frying pan with olive oil. The oil spit and hissed as the potatoes cooked, and within minutes, I was sampling a pancake with my fingers.

"This is really delicious," I said as I sucked air into my mouth to cool the bite.

"Of course it is!" Roger continued frying the potatoes for the other guests. "And now I have a very important question I want to ask you." He set down the spatula and looked into my eyes. "What is it that you want to master?"

The question took me by surprise, and I nearly choked on the potatoes.

"What do I want to master?" I asked, trying to buy myself time. "I'm not sure what you mean exactly."

"Everything is simple once you master it," he repeated. "I'm asking what you wish to master because there's something you're struggling with, and I'm sure you've been struggling for a long time. So my question is, how can you master it?"

I knew exactly what he meant and what he was trying to say, but I still wasn't ready to go to the chopping block so willingly. I could say that I wanted to master the guitar or to be a better writer . . . but that's not what he wanted, and I knew it.

"What makes you think I'm struggling with something?" I asked, hoping to evade the real question.

"We are all struggling with something." Roger picked up the spatula again and flipped the pancakes. "Yesterday morning, you were struggling with the fact that you were abandoned by someone you really cared for. She drove off and left you standing in the driveway like a sad dog, if I remember right. There must be something there, but if you don't want to talk about it . . ."

"No, I'll talk about it. Of course I will . . . that's why I'm here, right? I don't believe this is a coincidence, nothing like that. Michele could have left me anywhere, but she chose the one place where an enlightened French chef asks me all the questions I don't want to face."

"I'm definitely not—"

"*Enlightened?*" I interjected, knowing it wasn't in his nature to admit such a thing. "I guess it depends on what you think the word means. As far as I can tell, you're not only a master chef; you also have this way of imparting a pretty high degree of spiritual wisdom. It's no coincidence that I got dumped in your driveway, so I might as well play along."

"Good," he said. "Then tell me—what do you need to master?"

I took a long sip of coffee before answering.

"Your question implies that I'm here to master something that I'm struggling with," I finally said. "The most obvious thing right now is intimacy. On the one hand, I consider myself a really good person—the type of man any woman would love to be with. On the other hand, I can't seem to relax into a relationship long enough to let it settle in or form roots."

"How long has that been going on?" Roger asked.

"How long? As long as I can remember . . . definitely for several years now."

"So in one way or another you've felt it for a very long time," he replied as if he were homing in on something important, "but it's been much stronger the last few years. Why do you think that's happening?"

"You mean the last few years?"

As I asked this question, I could feel something inside my belly become dislodged, as if something that had been chained securely within me was now roaming freely about. Roger's words were like torpedoes aimed directly at the one thing I didn't want to look at, let alone talk about. Doing so would mean I'd have to *feel* it, and that was too scary, especially sitting there in Roger's kitchen.

"Yes," he said, pulling me back into the conversation. "Why do you think it's stronger now than before?"

I suddenly stood up and picked up my cup of coffee.

"I'm sorry, but I think I'm going to skip breakfast today," I hastily responded as I started to walk backward into the dining room.

"I'm not really feeling that well—I think I'll just hang out in my room for a bit."

As I turned around, I nearly ran into Kathleen, who was carrying several dishes from the dining room.

"Oh, I'm sorry!" she exclaimed as she expertly turned to the side and squeezed past me. "I just thought I'd bring these in. James, have you eaten yet?"

"I was just going to—"

"He was getting ready to," Roger interrupted. "James, do me a favor and sit in the dining room for a minute. I want to get the rest of the food ready for the couple, then I want to give you something. Is that okay?"

I looked into his eyes and felt such tenderness that there was nothing else for me to do.

"Yeah . . . I'll wait," I said, before walking slowly to the farthest table and sitting down. My head was spinning, and I wasn't sure why. Whatever had been loosened deep within me hadn't made its way to my conscious awareness. There seemed to be a wall between me and whatever it was, as if it were trying to keep me safe from what was on the other side.

I took several deep breaths hoping it would clear, but it didn't. The heaviness I felt when I first woke up that morning was now like a freight train lying directly on top of my body. I was being crushed by something I couldn't identify, even though it felt like the most intimate thing in my life.

Moments later, I saw Roger come out of the kitchen holding two plates, and he walked over to the older couple and set them down. He said a few words I couldn't really hear, then turned and walked toward me.

"Would you like more coffee?" he asked. "It would just take a minute."

"No, I think I'm okay," I answered, trying to stay composed.

Roger sat down next me. "I'm sorry if I hit a sore spot," he said. "I sensed there was something, but I didn't realize it was so deep. I didn't mean to push you."

"You didn't push me. And to tell you the truth, I don't even know what it is I'm feeling. Maybe it's just that Michele touched a raw nerve by leaving me, or maybe because I woke up this morning feeling out of sorts."

"Or maybe it's because you found the thing you're here to master," he offered, smiling. "It's usually the thing that scares us the most—that's how we know. If it were something simple and right on the surface, then it wouldn't be so difficult. I think the soul is always looking to be challenged because it needs to release the things that don't serve its higher goal . . . but it's never easy. Does that make sense?"

"It makes a lot of sense," I agreed. "Then again, I have no idea at this point. Something seems to have come loose inside me, and I don't even know what it is, but I do have the feeling it's the thing I've been running away from . . . probably what has been making me so afraid of intimacy."

"Why do you think you've been running away from it?" he asked.

"Probably because it's too painful to look at . . . or perhaps it's just the tip of the iceberg and God knows what is below the surface."

Kathleen walked out of the kitchen and stopped at the table.

"I need to do some stuff in the office," she said. "I'm not missing anything good, am I?"

Roger stood up and gave her a kiss.

"Darling, you never miss anything," he said. "That's why I love you so much, and it's why I married you."

It was as if his words created an avalanche inside me. I suddenly knew what I was hiding from—the thing I didn't want to look at because it would be too painful and require too much energy to heal. I turned away for a second, hoping my face didn't reveal what I was feeling. Roger gave Kathleen a final hug, and as she left the room, he sat back down and turned to me.

"Did I tell you that I was married once?" I asked. My voice felt heavy.

"No, I didn't know that," Roger replied.

"Linda and I met right after I finished college in 1984." I continued, "We were both twenty-two, and I had never actually been in a relationship before that. I remember so clearly the day we met because I thought she was the most beautiful woman I had ever seen. I was a goner within seconds, and I decided right then and there that I was going to marry her. I couldn't believe it when she later told me that she felt the same way—I was the luckiest guy in the world. About a year later, we were married, and before long we had our daughter, Angela. Things seemed to be going along just as I hoped.

"But I was too young and immature to make it work. I've beaten myself up about it a million times, but at the time I just wasn't ready for the responsibility. Linda and I eventually separated, and she gave up on me. You know, the funny thing was that we didn't finalize the divorce for about fifteen years because we were still really close friends, and also because I didn't want the marriage to end. I did everything I could to get her back, but sometimes when you push too hard . . .

"But then something seemed to shift. About six years ago, Linda decided that she wanted to join our daughter and me. Angela had moved to Oregon right after she finished high school, and I guess Linda was missing her. I was overjoyed, as you can imagine. I thought that maybe it was finally going to happen—even though I have no idea if it was something she even wanted. But it really did seem as if she was opening up to me in a whole new way. I thought that my dream of reuniting was finally going to come true."

"That's wonderful," Roger said. "But something must have happened."

I took a deep breath, not sure whether or not I could continue.

"Well, it was about two weeks later. I was on the phone with Linda, and we were making plans and talking about some of the details. I told her how excited I was, and she said she was excited, too. Maybe I was just hearing what I wanted to hear, but it felt like she was going to give us a chance. It had been almost eighteen years since we first separated, but it felt like everything was going to work out. Then the next morning, something really terrible happened."

The older couple had finished breakfast and walked over to the table without my even seeing them. The man touched Roger on the arm, and he turned toward them.

"Thank you so much for the lovely breakfast," the man said.

"Yes, it was perfect," his wife added. "I would love to sit down with you sometime and just pick your brain. You must have a million recipes in there."

"In a month, I'm going to be giving a cooking class here at Drew House," Roger said. "We have your address on file, so I'll make sure we send you the details so you can come."

"That would be lovely," the woman said.

"I think we're all taken care of with the bill," the husband told Roger. "We don't want to interrupt you, so don't worry about us at all."

"Thank you for coming, and I hope you'll visit us again," Roger said, smiling. He then turned back to me. "I'm sorry about that. You said something terrible happened the next morning . . ."

I could feel my fists clench beneath the chair, holding on to the wood as if it were a life raft. I didn't want to continue the story; I wanted to run out of the room and not stop till I was halfway to Toronto. Why did I let myself open that door? Did I really want to look at the single wound that had most impacted my life? Every dream and hope I've had, as well as every sorrow, was somehow wrapped inside this story. I had talked about it so many times that I never wanted to go there again, but there I was . . . and I knew there was nothing I could do but finish telling it.

"The next morning I found out that Linda had been murdered," I said to him. "I was in Minnesota, and my parents woke me up because they found out before I did. Angela was sleeping, and I had to tell her that she would never see her mother again. It's almost like a dream now, even though it's the worst dream I've ever experienced.

"So, you asked me what's been holding me back or making me afraid of intimacy. I guess that's it. I guess there's a place inside me that never wants to take that risk again, because I know how easily love can be ripped out of your life."

There should be some kind of warning system that alerts you when you're about to suffer the worst day of your life, I suddenly thought. There are sirens for the hurricanes and tornadoes that rip apart houses, but the tempests that tear apart lives usually approach unannounced. One minute you're asleep and dreaming, and then suddenly everything around you explodes, and the shrapnel tears through your life without warning. You look down at your hands and feet and wonder why you can't feel them, and then you realize that they're no longer attached in any recognizable way. Seconds later you understand what's really happening, that your hands and feet are fine—it was your heart that was blown to bits.

"First of all," Roger said as he reached across the table and touched my hand, "I want you to know how sorry I am that you went through something so terrible. I can't even imagine what it's like."

"And I hope you never do," I added. "It's the kind of thing you read about in the paper or see on the news, but not something you imagine actually happens to someone you know and love."

"Do they know who did it, or why?"

"Yes and no. They think they have at least one of the men who committed the crime, but they still have no idea why. There didn't seem to be a reason, which makes it even harder to deal with. When it's such a senseless act, it makes the experience far more difficult."

"Knowing all that," Roger said as he leaned back in his chair, "I have another question to ask. It may be something you're not ready to answer, and that's fine. But I want to at least bring it up in case you've come to a new point in your healing."

I took a deep breath, knowing that he was about to hit me with a question that could send me spinning out of control or in an entirely different direction. In the short time I'd spent with Roger, I had sensed that he was someone I could trust, and that he possessed a powerful insight into the human condition. I could resist it if I wanted to, but in that moment it seemed to make more sense to relax and let him guide me toward something I couldn't see myself.

"You're afraid to take the risk of loving someone because you know how easily it can be ripped from your life," he continued. "It makes a lot of sense and seems pretty understandable. Someone who has endured such trauma needs to create the space to grieve and really feel the loss. But how long do you really need before you're willing to trust love again—to know that love and loss are part of the same experience?

"You could spend the rest of your life running because you're afraid that you won't ever love someone like you loved Linda, and if you did, she might also be taken from you. But what kind of life would that be? If you ask me, it's not a full life at all, but a half life. There are probably millions of people in the world living that way, all because they lost something they held dear and were never able to heal. So, James, my question is: Are you ready to trust love again and open your heart? Before you answer, ask yourself whether or not you've gone through enough—and whether you've honored Linda's memory enough."

I felt a bolt of anger shoot through my body. *Had I honored her enough?* What kind of question was that? Of course I hadn't. I certainly hadn't honored her when I was twenty-five and threw away our marriage and everything we had created together. I hadn't honored her when I'd spent all those years building a career for myself when she was barely getting by and raising our daughter. I deserved everything I was feeling. It was my punishment, my self-imposed sentence for the sins I had committed against her.

"Listen," I said to Roger, "I get that you're trying to help, and I can appreciate what you're saying to me, but you really don't know what you're talking about. The fact is I could never go through enough to honor her. Even if I was sad for the rest of my life, it still wouldn't be enough."

"Then let me ask you one more question," Roger responded, holding the gentleness in his voice in a way that actually helped me release the anger I was feeling. "What do you think Linda would say if she were here right now? If she heard everything you said and was sitting with us at the table, do you think she would hold you responsible, or would she tell you that it's time to forgive yourself?"

"I know exactly what she would say," I replied, sitting back in my chair. "I know it because I experienced it. About a year ago, I had an experience—call it a dream or something much more real—where she was with me again. I was feeling the same thing, and she helped me see it in a different way. She does forgive me—I know that, but I also know that grief has so many layers, kind of like skin. You heal one layer and then the next layer presents itself, and you start all over."

"Just like the garlic," he said. "You've been smashed, and you can't pull the juice back inside anymore. Maybe you don't need to."

"What do you mean?" I asked him.

"Maybe you don't need to be the same person you were before all this happened. It's impossible. But you can be a more complete person, and that's a gift you can also give to others. Almost everyone has lost someone they love, and many of them also experience guilt and regret just like you do. You don't need to go backward or remain stuck; you need to find a way to take your experience and be of service."

"I've actually been trying to do that," I said as I finally released my grip on the chair. "To tell you the truth, the more I do, the easier it becomes. I actually wrote a book about my experience with Linda and was amazed by how many people resonated with it. So many people wrote to me, saying that my story helped them heal their own wounds. But then time goes by, and I find myself right back where I started, overwhelmed by guilt and unable to forgive myself, even though I thought I was done."

"We're never done," Roger remarked. "And that means we should never stop giving away the very thing we need most. It sounds like such a simple thing, but it's also the most powerful gift you can give yourself: The more you serve others, the more you receive."

"For it is in giving that we receive . . . and in loving that we are loved," I added.

"I've heard that before—though I'm not sure where."

"It's the Prayer of Saint Francis," I said. *"Grant that I may not seek to be loved as to love* . . . it's my favorite, and I think it makes a lot of sense in this situation."

"So that leads me back to something I asked you a little while ago," Roger continued. "What do you need to master in your life?"

The question seemed to make sense in a new way, as if the shades that had been drawn to block the light were suddenly pulled away, and sunlight came streaming into the room.

"I'm here to become a master of love," I finally said. "I can't believe I'm even saying this, but I think it's my greatest lesson. With everything that's happened—from Linda's death leading up to Michele driving away yesterday—I think it's telling me that I'm here to understand and really experience love in ways I didn't think were possible."

"What about when it becomes unbearable? What happens when everything inside you tells you to run and never look back?"

"I guess that's when I need to hold still and really look at myself—to find the place that's most afraid of love. I'm starting to see that this is where the greatest growth is, and it's the only way to master it. If I can just find the courage to face it, then little by little it begins to sink in, and I learn what I came here to understand."

Roger smiled. "So tell me, James . . . what did you come here to learn?"

"I came to learn about intimacy," I said, feeling naïve even though I knew I'd hit the nail on the head. "I guess that's what we're all here to learn about, but it's the trickiest thing in the world. . . ."

Far trickier than I could have ever imagined in that moment.

CHAPTER FOUR

Another Chance

I went to my room and let myself fall onto the bed. I just wanted to go to sleep and forget everything that had been stirred up. The last thing I needed was to think about Linda, the woman I had been mourning for years. At times the pain felt fresh, as if I'd just lost her; other times her memory would slip into a dark corner of my mind where I'd go to pray or hold silent benediction, as if she were an icon in a church. But when it came to taking down her image and replacing it with a real flesh-and-blood person—someone I could open my heart to—I flinched. This required much more risk, more than I felt capable of accepting.

As I was lying there, I thought about how much my trip had diverged from a romantic getaway with Michele to this purgatory. I was stuck somewhere between heaven and hell, and even though Roger was doing his best to show me the exit sign, I wasn't ready to leave. As uncomfortable as it was, I had grown used to the suffering; I actually enjoyed it. I realized that it was the first time I felt the grief momentarily leave me, as if I found myself on the edge of enjoying life again. But I was once again overcome by guilt and fear. I swatted away the flash of joy as if it were a sparrow that had flown in through an open window, and all I could think about was setting it free. It deserved its freedom, just as every creature of God does—but I was somehow different. For me it was an unthinkable luxury, one that I neither deserved nor hoped to enjoy.

I stared at the ceiling as my guilt came flooding back. I'd thought, or at least hoped, that I was ready to open my heart and that Michele was the woman who could sweep the cobwebs away, but I was wrong. Either I wasn't ready, or she wasn't the one . . . and it really didn't make a difference anyway.

There was something else I needed to acknowledge, something deeper and even more hidden that I didn't want to see or allow to resurface. An image began to form in my mind—of someone I had known and loved, but whom I'd turned away from just as I had turned away from Linda. Part of me didn't want to look—as if deep down I was aware of what I would discover about myself if I did—but then it rushed into my mind like water crashing over a levy, unable to hold back the tide. It was too late, so I relaxed and let the memory slowly unfurl like the ancient flag from a long-forgotten civilization buried beneath the sands of time and decay.

I'd known Nancy for about five years before we spent time together in Chicago. She was a well-known photographer from Montreal and had become a dear friend, but I never expected to fall in love with her. I was in the city visiting friends and heard that she was also in town attending a conference. We met for dinner because we hadn't seen each other for many months and wanted to catch up, and I sensed that something was different right away. It might have been the way she hugged me, not wanting to let go as quickly as before, or the way she looked into my eyes as we sat across from each other at the table. Something also came alive inside of me—a spark that found just the right environment to ignite a raging fire. It happened so fast I couldn't slow it down, and I didn't want to.

Nancy moved her chair closer to mine. She said it was so she could hear me better, but the restaurant wasn't noisy, and I sensed the real reason before she said a word. It began with our legs touching, almost as if we were testing each other. When I didn't pull away, she reached beneath the table and took my hand. Her touch felt so good, and it seemed that we were holding on with more power than needed—almost as if one of us were about to fall and we had to use all our strength to stop the inevitable plunge.

There was no way I could have known how accurate that analogy would turn out to be. How could I have seen that we were using one another to stop from falling off a cliff we couldn't even see? When we finally did see it, it was too late.

At this point, Linda had only been gone for about a year, and I was still reeling from the terrible shock of her death. The idea of dating another woman seemed foreign, even repulsive, but there was something about Nancy's energy that put me at ease. She was familiar and relaxed, which was what I needed, but there was something else . . . as if something had happened to her that put us at a similar disadvantage. I couldn't put my finger on it, especially since her mood was happy and light, but I knew it was there. Although I didn't feel ready, I was opening my heart without conscious intent. It was the first time I'd felt hopeful in many months, and I didn't see the need to dash it so soon.

"What's happening right now?" she asked in a voice that was so tender I couldn't resist moving closer to her.

"I really don't know. I had no idea this could happen."

"Anything can happen," Nancy said, "especially something like this. It comes out of nowhere; and when we least expect it, we discover something that's been in front of us for a very long time."

"Do you think this is possible?" I asked. "I'd like to believe so, because it feels amazing, but I have to admit it surprises me."

"Why does this surprise you?"

"Well, because I didn't think I was capable of feeling anything at all. Since Linda's death, I couldn't think of being open to anyone else, even though there's a really big part of me that would love to have the distraction. I knew that the only way to get through the grief is to stay open to the pain and anything else that wants to rise up inside me. It's been the most brutal thing I've ever experienced, but I never thought I had a choice."

"Of course you had a choice," she said as she squeezed my hand. "We always do. You have a choice right now, too; and to me, it feels like you're choosing the same thing I am."

"And exactly what is that?" I asked. "I mean, I think I know, but I want to hear it from you."

"We're choosing to be open—maybe because we need it right now. I know why you need it, and I also need it . . . but in a different way."

"Can you tell me why you need this? I don't want to pry, but I want to know where you are and what's brewing inside you."

Nancy let go of my hand and turned away just enough to pick up her glass of wine and take a sip. I knew I had said too much and had hit a nerve. I hoped I could find a way to help her recover before she had the chance to reconsider what was happening between us.

"I don't want to say anything more about that," she said without looking up at me. "I will, but I'm not quite ready."

I reached out and took her hand again, and the movement was enough to get her to look away from the table and back into my eyes.

"I don't know what's happening, Nancy, and I won't try to get you to tell me until you're ready. But I do want you to know that it feels pretty amazing sitting here with you right now. I don't need any answers, and I definitely don't need any guarantees, but I hope you know that I'm here for you in any way you need me."

"I know that, and I do trust you. I'll tell you what's going on very soon. In fact, I feel like I need to talk to someone. If I don't, I might just go crazy."

It was springtime, and the weather in Chicago was magnificent. We left the restaurant and found a park where we could walk and hopefully continue the conversation. The excitement I felt made it difficult to defend the part of myself that wanted to hide and not risk feeling anything for her, or for anyone else.

A year felt like a long time to go without even the consideration of any romantic involvement, but I knew I couldn't force myself. I always figured that it would happen on its own . . . that one day I would wake up and feel different, or that someone would appear to make me feel ready. That was exactly what seemed to be happening with Nancy, and although it felt too soon, the last thing I wanted to do was push her away.

"I've been having some health challenges," she said as we walked arm in arm, and I could feel her body pull back slightly from mine. There was a long pause, and I wondered if I should fill in the space or wait for her to continue.

"What kind of challenges?" I finally asked when it became clear that she wasn't going to give me more unless I coaxed it out of her. She stopped walking and looked into my eyes. She was holding both of my hands, and the street lamp behind me gently shone down on her, making her seem more like an angel as she stood there gazing at me.

"I have cancer," Nancy replied. "Breast cancer. I found out about a month ago, and I've been trying to decide what to do."

"What to do?" I gently squeezed her hand. "What choices do you have?"

"My doctor wants me to begin treatment right away—all the normal stuff they do when you have something like this. But I don't think I want to. I want to treat it holistically . . . diet, exercise, that kind of thing. I don't trust medicine or the doctors who prescribe it. There are a lot of people who have overcome cancer without having a single chemo treatment."

I took a step back so I could see her clearly; I also wanted her to see the concern in my face.

"Nancy, there's nothing wrong with trying alternative treatments, but why can't you do both? I've known many people who have balanced the two. I don't think it's wise to turn your back on something that could save your life. You have two young daughters to think about."

She turned away and the expression on her face immediately changed. She was no longer the happy, lighthearted woman I had been sharing the evening with. Her eyes turned dark, and I felt her energy and body contract.

"That's what everyone has been saying," she said flatly, "but it's not what feels right to me. *I* believe in miracles, and that's what I'm going to create."

"You're not hearing what I'm saying," I said, in a more urgent tone. "I *want* you to believe in miracles, and I *want* you to do all the healthy things you're talking about. But why do you have to turn your back on—"

"Listen, James. I'm not going to talk to you about this if you're not going to support me. That's why I don't tell many people, because then I have to deal with all their judgments, and they get inside my head."

"But they're not being judgmental. It's common sense. And I feel a little guilty saying this, but I really want you to be around. Maybe it's selfish, but I feel like there's something happening between us, and I don't want it to stop."

"Why would it stop? The only thing that would stop it would be you trying to force me to do something I don't want to do."

I stepped forward and took hold of her hands, hoping to calm her down so I could approach the conversation from a different angle.

"I'm not going to do anything like that, Nancy. Believe me. But let me ask you this: how much of your conviction is based on other people thinking they know what's best for you?"

She took a deep breath and seemed to relax. Then she looked up at me, and the gentleness returned to her face.

"I don't know," she replied. "Of course, everyone's been saying the same thing because they care and are worried, but there's something inside that is urging me to go in a different direction. I can't seem to deny it or push it away. I have this feeling that if I can heal the cancer naturally, I'll be an example to so many others who will make the same choice. I almost feel like it's my service or a ministry that will help others."

It quickly became clear that there was nothing I could do to sway her. I wanted Nancy to think of me as her ally, not someone she had to argue with. The energy I was feeling between us needed the chance to grow, but it somehow shifted. I started to feel more like a man who had been lost in the desert, dying of thirst. A beautiful oasis was right in front of me, but as soon as I reached out, it vanished before my eyes. A mirage.

"I told you before that I'm here for you," I said, "and I meant it. I promise to honor and support whatever you decide. I can't imagine how difficult this must be for you, and I definitely don't want to make it any harder than it already has been."

I held her all night, hoping that I wasn't putting myself into another painful situation I couldn't endure. As I lay in bed with her, I looked up at the ceiling and saw Linda's face in every shadow. The darkness was still in my mind and wasn't going to disappear after a single night, but there was something else I was trying to push away.

What would happen if I really did open up to Nancy and give my heart the chance to feel deep love? What if I surrendered to the excitement and passion . . . and then she died? Was I capable of losing someone else? How much could a person endure? A day earlier, I hadn't even thought it was possible to love another woman when I was still so broken, but all that had changed when I saw Nancy. What if she was resolute in her decision and chose to battle the disease without a doctor? What if she *lost* the battle? Would I die along with her?

I went back to Oregon two days later, and we decided to stay in close contact. We would explore being in a relationship and see how we could make that work. Of course, distance was an issue, but Nancy was even considering moving to the West Coast to be with me. At first it seemed like a great idea, and I was tremendously excited by the possibilities. On the other hand, no matter how hard I tried, I couldn't seem to shake my fears. I was careful about how I spoke about the cancer, but in spite of what everyone said, Nancy remained committed to handling her treatment in her own way.

A month passed, and I found myself calling her less often and not answering the phone when I saw her number on the caller ID. Before long, we were speaking once a week, and even then I knew she could sense my distance. I wanted her to confront me on it, to ask what was wrong or even become furious—anything to shake me from my indecision. Instead, she seemed complacent, almost as if she preferred to be by herself. By the time summer had arrived, the closeness we'd developed had vanished, and I was alone again.

We spoke every month or so, but neither of us mentioned the two days we'd spent together in Chicago. It was like it had never happened, and although the connection between us still existed, we only allowed ourselves to dwell on the surface where the fear—as well as the tenderness—was held in check. Nancy spent long weeks isolated and alone, not answering her phone or e-mails. The distance made me feel even more cut off than before, yet there was nothing I could do but wait and see what happened next.

Nancy remained steadfast in her decision not to seek traditional medical treatment, and within six months, the cancer had spread throughout her entire body. I heard from a mutual friend that she had finally gone back to her doctor, but by then it was too late. I wanted to call her, but every time I picked up the phone I couldn't seem to dial the number. My heart was reaching out to her, but I also felt like I had abandoned the one woman who could have delivered me from the nightmare I had endured since Linda's death. If I had treated her as she deserved, then perhaps she would have realized what she needed to before it was too late. If I'd had the courage to stand strong and hold her no matter what she decided, then maybe the miracle she was hoping for would have found us both.

I heard that Nancy had died from our mutual friend Tara. She called one afternoon crying and said that Nancy had passed away peacefully, surrounded by her children. I set the phone down and stared off into space for a very long time. I could almost feel her body next to me again, just as I'd felt it that night. Once again, I sensed that I had chosen wrong and that what had happened was my fault. Whether or not that was true, my body absorbed the blow and waited for more to come.

Strike two.

CHAPTER FIVE

The Intensity You Bring to Life

As I opened my eyes and looked around the room, I suddenly realized that I had fallen asleep. Several years had passed since I had seen Nancy, and yet I wasn't at all surprised to feel her spirit still hovering about. Like the scent of a beautiful bouquet of flowers that lingers in the room long after it's been removed, her face drifted through my mind with greater persistence than I thought possible. Rolling over to look at the clock, I saw that it was 1:00 P.M. I had been sleeping for two and a half hours. Then I heard a sound coming from the hallway, a low motorized hum that increased as the seconds passed, which I assumed was the maid vacuuming. I hopped up, wanting to get moving before the maid came to the door with the vacuum cleaner. Walking to the bathroom, I turned on the light and splashed water on my face. Seconds later, I was heading downstairs, hoping I wouldn't see anyone I knew, since starting a conversation was the last thing I needed. What I wanted was to get outside and clear my head . . . hopefully find a way to hold the ghosts of my past at bay so I could catch my breath.

I stood in the driveway where Michele had left me the previous morning and watched the scene again in my mind. The sun was brighter than it had been, and the temperature was warm enough to walk around without a jacket. I looked in the direction she had driven and decided to follow the path, almost as if I would find her waiting around the corner. As I walked, I thought about Linda and Nancy and every other woman I'd run from over the years. My footsteps felt heavy as their faces appeared, one after another, and I increased my stride, hoping to outrun them all. Then I stopped, as if the energy was unexpectedly drained from my body. A thought, or perhaps a realization, was forming that I hadn't considered before. Part of me wanted to push it away, as if I had done enough for one day. The other, greater part of me wanted to at least see what it was, allowing it the room to breathe and express whatever insight it could offer.

It was at that very moment that I realized I was very similar to Nancy—my "disease" was less obvious, though, and not fatal. Like Nancy, I had also refused to accept the help I was offered to overcome the effects of the malady, choosing instead to *go it alone* and hope for the best. And because I had waited too long, it had spread through my whole body, seeping in through the cracks of my existence and infecting every person I let into my life.

Was it too late to turn the tide and approach life from a new direction—one that would rebuild and heal the foundation that seemed to be crumbling beneath me? If it wasn't, then I wanted to at least try. I didn't want to continue the cycle that was spinning me in directions I no longer wanted to go. I was ready for change, and I instinctively knew I was in the perfect place to usher it in.

I heard a horn honk and turned to see who it was. Roger's truck pulled up next to me, and he rolled down the window.

"Are you out for a walk, or do you want a ride home?" he asked. I wondered if I was ready to open the door and get in, knowing that if I did, he would likely challenge me to look at other issues I'd been avoiding. Thanks to Roger, I was already spread out on the chopping block like the garlic he pounded into submission. What was the point in trying to evade more punishment, since it seemed to be transforming my life with such proficiency?

I opened the door and stepped into the car.

"I was enjoying this beautiful day," I lied. "Everything seems vibrant, and I guess it was what I needed."

"Why did you need that?" he asked, and I could already feel the lesson beginning.

"Well, our talk this morning got me thinking about things I've ignored for some time. But I do need to look at them—I know that now, but it's really hard. I guess I should thank you."

"There's no reason to thank me," Roger replied. "You're the one who's being brave, overturning the rocks where your fears have been hiding. I'm just asking the questions because that's what I do. I'm nosey!"

"I don't think you're nosey at all, but I do think you have a unique ability to dive into people's heads and know what they're hiding from. I just wonder how that works at a party. . . ."

"It never works very well," he answered, smiling, having understood my joke. "People usually run away when they see that look in my eye—the one that says I'm going to penetrate their armor and make them feel the things they don't want to feel. After a few glasses of wine, it can get pretty ugly."

I laughed at the thought of him at a party, engaged in the same type of deep discussions we'd been having. It helped to lift the energy surrounding my memories of Linda and Nancy, and I felt myself relax.

"If it wasn't so early, I'd love a glass of wine," I said. "Things have been pretty intense since I arrived."

Roger pulled up to Drew House and parked the truck, and I followed him around to the back to help carry the groceries.

"You do realize that you're getting to the heart of what's truly important in life, don't you?"

"I didn't think of it in that way," I replied, "but I have the feeling I'm about to find out how that's true."

We walked into the kitchen and set the bags on the counter. Then Roger looked at me and smiled.

"Okay, here's the one thing that's truly important in life: the universe only pays attention to the intensity you bring to it. That's why it's good that things are intense for you right now. As long as you have integrity, courage, and the ability to put your whole heart into whatever you do, then everything will ultimately turn out for the best. That's the sole thing that God, or the universe, looks for."

"The intensity you bring to life . . ." I repeated, as I started taking things out of the bags and setting them in piles, based on which items went into the refrigerator and which were meant for the cupboard. "But *intensity* can mean different things. What if someone's intensity turns out to be destructive? That can't be good, right? What if that person does things that end up hurting others?"

"Ah, now you've raised a very interesting point," Roger noted. "Let me see if I can explain it better. Another word for intensity is *passion*. In order for your passion to really benefit you, you have to add one more ingredient: service. Do you remember when we were making Rösti potatoes, and I told you that the eggs held it all together? Imagine if you didn't add the eggs—it would fall apart, right? It would break up in the pan, and I wouldn't be able to serve it. That's what I'm trying to explain. Passion is useless if you don't direct it into serving others. It ultimately falls apart. It has to move from you to another before it can return to you again. If you're only passionate about the things that are for you, then you can't be replenished.

"Think of it in this way," he continued. "A robber may have a great passion for stealing, but it eventually leads to destruction—one way or another. Why? Because a crook takes from another to give to himself. He's not serving; he's using his passion to serve himself, and at some point, it's going to end. It can't sustain itself forever."

"What about Robin Hood?" I asked. "He was stealing from the rich but giving to the poor."

"Very good point. Robin Hood wasn't doing it just to get rich himself, was he? He was acting to serve his entire community. He was also teaching a lesson to the people who try to hoard their wealth and don't think about the less fortunate."

"Does the word *crook* come from *crooked?*" I wondered aloud, not really sure where the thought came from.

"Yes, I think it does, and that leads to another way of understanding this lesson. If something is crooked, then the energy can't move in a straight line. The most efficient path is the shortest and most direct, right? So the more you serve others, the straighter the energy moves toward fulfilling your own needs and desires, as well as the needs and desires of others. Whatever gift you give to another is really a gift to yourself. Obviously, people have been saying that for centuries, but most still don't listen. They think that life is about serving themselves and getting what they think they deserve. But what if the answer really is this simple: *Give what is inside you, and it increases.* It would be revolutionary if everyone just decided to live in this way."

"It all comes back to keeping things simple," I added.

"Yes, it does. The goal is always *outside.* Now that may sound like I'm contradicting myself because I said before that it's all within. Both are true for one very important reason: you cannot know what is within you until you put it *outside*—that is, until you give it away. In order for it to really serve, it has to move from the inside to someone else, not the other way around. Is it enough to accumulate stuff, or be the smartest or the best at something? Release it, and you'll be even better than before; hoard it for yourself and it starts to go crooked because the energy isn't flowing. That's what *I've* learned, anyway, and I try to live it in simple ways, especially when I cook . . . as I'm about to do now."

"Are people coming for dinner tonight?" I asked.

"No one, except for you, and I would like to make something special. I hope you don't mind—"

". . . mind if you make me something special? How could I ever complain about that!"

"One more thing . . ." Roger added. "Although it seems like I know what I'm talking about, the fact is that I'm continually learning just like you are—and everyone else. Do you remember when we were at the farm stand yesterday, and I told the woman that you were my teacher? I meant it. You're giving me the chance to share some of the things that make sense to me. If I don't share it, I forget all of it. That's the gift you've given me—the chance to remember."

An hour later I was back in my room wondering how everything fit together, especially given the strange circumstances I found myself in. A day earlier I thought I'd never stop repeating the same destructive pattern. It was as if I kept hitting a wall, yet I never seemed to notice until I was bruised and lying flat on my back. Then Roger came into my life and pushed a button only he could see, and I started remembering the most difficult lessons of them all: Linda and Nancy. My experiences with them had a common thread, and I sensed that if I could figure it out, I would be well on my way toward healing. It was a good theory, so I decided to stick with it.

I dialed Michele's number, hoping she would be willing to talk, but then I froze. What was I going to say? Did I want her to come back to Drew House, or have her ask me to join her in Toronto? I took a deep breath and realized that I had to trust my instincts. I was exactly where I needed to be, and, at the moment, that meant spending as much time as I could sitting on a stool in a little kitchen in Elora. I knew I could face the real lesson there, whatever it was, and perhaps if I was lucky, I'd break through to the other side.

In any case, I decided to call Michele and see what would transpire.

"I didn't think I'd pick up if you called," Michele said before I even had the chance to say hello. "The only reason I did was because I feel guilty for having abandoned you all the way out there. How did you get back to Toronto?"

"I didn't," I replied. "Believe it or not, I'm still at Drew House. I'd planned to leave, but something is happening to me here, so I think I'm going to stay a bit longer."

"What do you mean? Why didn't you just get a taxi or rent a car? When are you planning to leave?"

"To tell you the truth, I don't really know. Do you remember Roger, the French guy who owns the place? We started talking right after you took off, and it turns out he's some kind of spiritual mystic as well as a chef. He has sort of taken me under his wing, helping me see a few things."

There was a long pause on the other end of the line, and for a second, I wondered if Michele was still there. Then I heard her take a deep breath before continuing.

"Leave it to you to come out smelling like a rose," she finally said. "Do you realize I cried almost the whole way back home? I don't understand why you changed and made me feel so alone, even though you were right next to me."

"That's exactly what I'm trying to figure out. I had no idea I was doing anything like that. As far as I knew, you and I were having a great time, and then we were suddenly heading in different directions. I think I'm finally starting to see something about myself that I've never noticed. That being said, I was hoping you would answer a question for me."

I took a deep breath before continuing. "From the time we spent together, would you describe me as a happy person?"

I'm not really sure where the question came from. I felt it brewing inside me every time I was with Roger, and even though I never thought of myself as unhappy or discontent, I was wondering if there was something deep within, other than the obvious, that was blocking my happiness. I was successful in my career, which allowed me to travel around the world speaking and writing—the kind of thing most people dream of. From the outside, my life looked amazing, and although I've been adept at blocking the real reason I've been hiding from love, it seemed to be seeping out in ways I didn't see and certainly couldn't stop.

"Well, let me put it this way," Michele said. "You give the appearance of being a happy person, but deep down there's an impatience about you that never lets you hold still. It's like you're always wondering what's around the corner, or where your escape route might be if something better comes along. It's subtle, but I started to notice it on this trip.

"When we first met, you were so focused on getting my attention, but as soon as you had it, it was like you needed to move on to something else. I don't know if that makes you unhappy or if it's something deeper. I suspect it's something you haven't even touched yet, and you probably won't until you just hold still."

It was as if her words ignited an open gas line inside me, and I felt an explosion of energy. No one had ever put it so succinctly before, in a way I was able to truly hear . . . even though I never wanted to hear it. Was I really as restless as Michele said I was? Was I going to run from the feelings that were surfacing in Elora, the very ones that had pushed me into an emotional shell since losing Linda and Nancy? And if I was, what role did Michele play in all of it? Our relationship was still young and had made very little of the impact I had experienced with the others; on the other hand, she seemed more like a catalyst for me—an angel who had been sent to open the door a bit wider so that I would once and for all see who I was and what I was doing.

"I think that's why I'm here at Drew House," I continued. "I was supposed to hold still for a moment, and as soon as I did, surprising things started coming to the surface. I never intended to hurt you, but until I finally deal with the issues running through my heart, it will likely continue with the next person and the one after that. It needs to stop here. I need to stop it. It's time for me to trust love again and feel like I deserve to be loved in return."

"Of course you deserve it," Michele said. "We all deserve love, but not everyone is willing to do what it takes to welcome it. It takes courage to go there, and it's never as neat and tidy as we want it to be."

"I don't want it to be neat and tidy, but I do want it to be real. Since you left and I've been hanging out with Roger, I've gained a lot of perspective. One of the things he's helped me see is that I'll never heal if I stay focused on what I think I need, or the things I believe I want. That's what I've been doing, even though on the surface I've been doing the opposite. I spend all my time talking about service and love, but I can't seem to do it myself. I thought maybe you could help me with that. . . ."

It was a fainthearted attempt to draw Michele back in, hoping she would feel my remorse and drive back to Elora. But was that really what I wanted: a second chance? Or was I right where I needed to be? She said that I was incapable of holding still—restless and unable to be truly present with anyone. As much as I hated to admit it, her words struck a chord inside me that I had never felt before. If it was true, and if Michele really wasn't the cure, then reconciling with her so soon was just repeating the same pattern as before. I held my breath waiting for her answer, almost hoping she wouldn't take the bait I had thrown in her direction.

"You don't need my help," she replied. "You need yourself—not me. I'm not saying that I never want to see you again. I have to admit that I was overly dramatic yesterday, leaving you stranded, but that's over now. If you need a ride, I'll be happy to come get you, but it will only be to take you to the airport so you can go home. If you want my opinion, I think you should just stay put. It seems like you're getting something you need, so why rush the process? If Roger is helping you see something about yourself, then you might as well take a good look. You never know what you'll learn."

And with that, the conversation ended. Michele was right, of course, just as Roger was right, and just as I was right about wanting to hold still . . . if only for a couple more days. Something was shifting inside me, and I didn't want it to stop. It was a rather uncomfortable feeling, but I knew that real growth is never easy.

Around 7 o'clock, I heard Roger call up the stairs.

"James? Dinner will be ready in about five minutes. Come down whenever you want."

I had been playing my guitar for the last half hour, something that usually puts me at ease, especially when I'm feeling overwhelmed. Part of me wanted to stay upstairs and give my mind a rest, but I knew I had opened a door that I couldn't suddenly close. If I did, I would likely end up in far worse shape than I was at the moment, which was definitely something I didn't want. So I opened my door and stepped into the hallway, then walked down the stairs. There was no reason to put it off or think that Roger would go easy on me this evening. I was beginning to learn that "going easy" wasn't something he knew how to do very well.

"Hi, James! How was your day?"

It was Kathleen who asked the question, and I wondered how honest I should be with her. I wanted to tell her that her husband had thrown me into the deep end of the pool without teaching me how to swim. Rather, it would be more accurate to say that he had tossed me into the deep end of the kitchen, the place where someone like Roger thrives but an amateur like me sinks like a stone. I had learned the best way to make coffee and how to make a wicked potato pancake, but the only thing that really mattered was the way Roger had taught me to smash garlic. It was the perfect metaphor, except in reality, it was *me* being squashed, not the garlic.

"My day was active," I replied. "Lots of stuff going on—more than I expected, but overall, I'm very good. How about you?"

"Lots going on for me, too. We're going on a little vacation soon—right around Thanksgiving—so I've been trying to get everything organized. It's also going to be a busy holiday season in Elora, although we won't have too many guests at Drew House. There are so many events and parties planned, and we also have one of Roger's cooking classes in December. You should come back for that, James. People really love it, and Roger does a great job teaching the things he knows, and cooking French cuisine, of course. When I say 'the things he knows,' . . . well, I'm guessing you understand that by now."

I wanted to respond that when I did finally leave, it would be a long time before I would return, due to my busy schedule, but also because part of me hoped my life would return to normal—the way it was before I'd met Roger. And that was the real question: when would I be allowed to leave? Obviously, I wasn't being held hostage, and if I was, I couldn't think of a better place for that to happen. It was more about why I was here and knowing that I couldn't go until I finished whatever I had started.

On the other hand, Roger and Kathleen felt like good friends I had known my entire life; we already shared a level of intimacy that isn't easy to find. I could see myself coming back again and again, even if it was just to learn more about cooking so I could impress my friends who didn't think I could fry an egg.

Roger walked into the room carrying a large serving dish filled with something I couldn't identify, but the smell was enough to send me over the edge. I hadn't realized how hungry I was until that very moment, and I was anxious to know what was awaiting us.

"Tonight we're having paella," Roger said as he set the platter onto the table. "It's a Spanish dish and I'm a French cook, but since the Basque people live in both France and Spain, I thought it would be okay for tonight."

"It smells amazing!" I exclaimed.

"Roger is known for his seafood dishes," Kathleen said to me, "especially his fish soup. He won a prestigious award here in Canada called the Golden Whisk; it was actually for his beef bourguignon. The funny thing is that Roger is a vegetarian—rather, a pescetarian since he does eat fish. He doesn't eat red meat, but he still won this big national award for his meat dish!"

"It's true that I'm better known for what I can do with fish," Roger added. "It's partly because I always like to prepare things fresh, when there's still a strong life force. As I've said, everything has a life force, and if you take it away, it has very little benefit. I guess you could say that we're here to ingest life in many, many ways—not just the way we eat, of course, but in the way we breathe and how we live. The more life we welcome, the more life welcomes us."

"You should write that down, James," Kathleen said to me. "I don't think I've ever heard him say that before, and it's a pretty good line."

"If I ever use it in a book, I'll be sure to give you credit," I told them with a smile as I sat down at the table. There was already a beautiful salad and a plate of cooked vegetables waiting for us, and Roger poured me a glass of red wine.

"Bon appétit," Roger said, smiling, as we lifted our glasses for a toast. "They thought I was pretty brave making the beef bourguignon. It really wasn't anything at all—just a recipe I've used for years. The secret is to flambé the wine to reduce the acidity. But you must have a gas stove; it's the only way to get the temperature high enough to ignite the wine."

"How did you get so good at making fish soup?" I asked him as I eyed the paella. I wanted to finish my salad as quickly as possible so I could move on to the main course.

"Well, living by the sea taught me how to recognize the best and freshest seafood," he replied. "My first restaurant was a place right on the water near my home. It was small and we only served a few dishes—my fish soup was one of them—so I became very good at it.

"Years later when I was in New York, I found a restaurant that specialized in Basque cuisine; they even had this enormous painting of my hometown on the wall right where I was sitting. I told the owners that it was where I was raised, and they couldn't believe it. That gave me the idea to do something similar here in

Toronto—to open a restaurant specializing in the food I was raised with. In the end, I had a small chain in the city before I sold them all and moved to Australia."

I finished my salad and spooned a healthy amount of rice onto my plate, then covered it with the incredible-smelling main dish. The cod and salmon seemed to pop with freshness and life, and the clams made the entire dish perfect.

"I'm very impressed," I said to Roger. "Obviously, I'm not a foodie, but this is one of the best things I've ever tasted."

"If I try to impress someone with my cooking, it never turns out well," Roger remarked. "I think of food as a way to love the individuals I'm cooking for. It's a simple idea, but it transforms everything, and people feel it whether or not they consciously know it. If I put every ingredient I have into a dish I'm preparing, trying to do too much, then the original energy or intent gets lost—no one can taste it because there's too much going on.

"It's like being with someone you love. Is it better to tell her with as few words as possible how you feel, or overwhelm her with poetry and prose and all the other ways you can express yourself? When I want to tell Kathleen how much I love her, then I do it as simply as I can. I *show* her. The same is true when I'm cooking. I'm not here to overwhelm anyone, but to communicate something through food—something that only comes when I strip the recipe down to the most essential ingredients."

"I've been to workshops where presenters spend all their time talking about how much they know," Kathleen added. "And the participants are impressed for a few moments, but if you ask them what they learned a day, or even an hour, later, they really can't tell you. I've also studied with teachers who don't say much at all, but they lead you into an experience that has nothing to do with words or concepts. They help you find the answers within yourself instead of just giving them to you. If you ask people what they got from the experience, they'll go on for an hour describing the way they felt or how it changed their lives. I think that's the key: if you keep it simple and don't add too much of your own self-interest to the mix, then people feel the energy that's beneath the surface."

"That's one of the reasons why I'm really glad I'm a musician," I said in between bites of paella. "I love to teach, but so many people have told me that when I sing, it goes straight to the heart. I think it's because I can actually feel it coming from a different place inside me. I'm *feeling* as opposed to *thinking.* I also feel like I've successfully gotten out of my own way. Does that make sense? It's not coming *from* me, but *through* me because I am able to surrender what I want to happen into what actually is happening. If I can accomplish that when I'm with an audience or at a church or wherever, then I feel like I've done my job."

"It doesn't matter whether you're cooking or singing," Roger said. "It's all the same thing: it has to come from your heart and from a desire to love the people you're serving. That being said, I just want you to know how happy we are that your friend left you stranded here with us, James. It's an unexpected surprise, and it has given me the chance to flex a few muscles I haven't used in a while."

"What muscles are you talking about?" I asked.

"You remind me of myself at certain times in my life," he replied. "We all go through periods when we don't know what our next move is, or we've come to the end of the road and have to choose a new route. I've been there many times, even to the point of wondering if I would continue as a chef. But then something happens, or someone comes along, to remind me of what's important, and I get myself back on track. In some ways, I'm just returning the favor—giving you a gift that was given to me many times before."

"Well, I'm glad I'm here, too," I said to both of them. "I can't quite say that I'm happy I was dumped and left on your doorstep, but at the same time, I think it was exactly what I needed. I've uncovered things that I was afraid to look at, and now that I have, I'm starting to view them in new ways. . . ."

"I have no idea what the two of you are talking about," Kathleen said, "but it sounds interesting. I'm not surprised, though. When Roger's in the kitchen doing his thing, all sorts of miracles happen."

"I believe it," I said. "I'd be surprised if I was the first."

CHAPTER
SIX

Sister, Forgive Me

"I started telling you about my mother and family two days ago," Roger said, "and how I became interested in being a chef."

It was early in the afternoon, the day after I enjoyed Roger's amazing dinner, and I went looking for him after a long walk to the Elora Gorge. I found him in the kitchen prepping for a meal he was planning to serve the following night for a local women's group. Although he did his best to discourage requests to create lavish banquets and dinner parties, now and then some of the community's organizations and businesses would persuade him, as these women had, and he found himself back in a very familiar role.

Earlier in the day, though, I'd enjoyed a nice walk and some time with my thoughts. I'd woken up with the feeling that it was time to sort through the voices and deafening echoes that were swimming through my head, many of which I'd been ignoring for years, or even decades. *What did I need to hear?* The more I walked, the deeper they seemed to penetrate my consciousness, and I wanted to absorb as much as I could before I left the next day.

My exit from Drew House would be quite different from what I'd imagined when I first arrived, but I also realized that I had received much more than I'd hoped for. I thought I came to explore a relationship with Michele, but it became more of a self-exploration: learning to love the parts of myself I had neglected or ignored, hoping they would heal on their own or disappear. Instead, they were the lead weights slowing my progress. But now these aspects of myself were on the surface—a place where they could finally be seen and addressed—and although it was disconcerting, I sensed that I was indeed growing and evolving in positive ways.

"I thought what you were telling me was fascinating," I said to Roger. "Especially about your mother being part of the French Resistance."

"You know, the BBC gave her the code name *Mouton Blanc,* or 'White Sheep.' Her family called her their 'Parisian white sheep' because she looked so different from them. Of course, she didn't resemble anyone else because she was adopted. Do you remember the story I told you earlier? That my mother's birth mother became pregnant out of wedlock, and her family sold the illegitimate child—my mother—rather than be shamed?

"Well, it wasn't until after my mother's death that I found out something shocking while I was at a family reunion. One of my elderly aunts was telling stories. She revealed that not long after my mother was born, both her birth mother and father, who was a Polish soldier, committed suicide. Can you imagine? I was stunned, of course, and always wondered how my mother must have felt. Did she think she was the cause of the tragedy? Had she even known what had happened to her birth parents? It's so strange when you look back at the stories that shape your life, or the lives of the people you love."

It was beginning to feel normal: the way in which Roger would home in on the exact issue I was wrestling with. I had been reflecting on my past more than I had in my entire life, and although I didn't always like what I saw, there was a movement or progression I couldn't deny. Until then I always seemed to be going in reverse, as if trying to unhinge something I had yet to perceive, but now it felt like I had finally shifted gears and was moving forward . . . perhaps a bit faster than I wanted to.

"It's funny you would mention that," I said as I sat down on my familiar stool. "I was talking to Michele yesterday, and she helped me see how my own stories and history have shaped the way I am— like the fact that I tried so hard to save my marriage and make up for the mistakes I made when I was younger. Then when it looked like I was finally going to have the chance I'd been longing for, it was destroyed. When Linda was killed, I think something inside me died, too. I don't think I realized that until yesterday, or even today."

"So what will you do with it now?" Roger asked.

"What can I do? Maybe I just admit that it's there and try to change."

"I guess what I'm asking is how will you change? You aren't going to do anything by feeling guilty. That just makes the wound deeper. Maybe there's a way you can help others who have been going through similar struggles. If you could be of service to someone else, then healing will take place on its own."

"How can something like that help others?" I inquired.

"I don't know. That's up to you to decide. All I know is that sometimes God wants you to play a certain role, but if you turn your back on it, He finds other ways to push you in that direction. And you often find that it's not so pleasant when you don't listen. . . .

"I remember once I was on the Caribbean island of St. Martin with Kathleen. I think it was in 2005. During our third night there, I woke up from the most amazing dream. It was so vivid, so real, that I had to tell Kathleen about it right away. You might think this is very strange, James, but I have the feeling I'm supposed to tell you about this. Anyway, there was a beautiful being made out of light that appeared to me, and his presence filled me with awe. He spoke to me for some time, saying that I would write a book based on a single line that was seared into my mind: *You are the result of what you think and eat.* That was it. This being told me that one day I would share this insight with the world."

"Was it something you've heard before?" I asked him. "I've heard a similar idea but in different words."

"Yes. In fact, I'd heard the exact same thought before—from Edgar Cayce, someone you might be familiar with."

"Oh yes . . . he was called the Sleeping Prophet because he would go into a trance and give readings to people, often telling them about their lives or how they could be healed from different ailments."

"Exactly!" Roger exclaimed as he became more exited. "He said the exact same thing in one of his readings, out of many thousands that were recorded. Well, after some time the dream began to fade, and I started to think it was a crazy idea. Who was I to write a book and share this notion? I put it out of my mind and moved on with my life."

"I have the feeling I know where this is going," I added.

"You probably do. Like I said, when God gives us something to do for the world, it's vital that we pay attention. If we ignore it, we sometimes receive a dramatic reminder. For me, it began a short time later, when I started to resent my career as a chef. I had always loved what I do, but something seemed to have changed. I actually wanted to give it all up! Believe it or not, I woke up the next day with painful shingles all over my body, but I kept on pushing. The pain grew worse, and I finally went to the doctor.

"Well, my doctor was telling me different things, unable to help me, and then I had an epiphany. I decided it was time to renew my commitment to the book I was told about in the dream. Once I made the decision, my body seemed to respond immediately. The pain stopped a few hours later, and when I went back to see my doctor, everything was fine. This showed me that I was destined to share this message."

"Did you actually write the book?"

"I did write it, and I've been waiting for the right moment to do something with it. I know it's just a matter of time because this is such an important message. It's significant because we really are what we think and what we eat. Many people believe that our thoughts create our reality, but they don't understand how vital the food we put into our bodies is. There is a correlation. The two play such key roles, and that's the message I'm committed to sharing."

"I'm having a difficult time seeing how this plays into what I'm experiencing, though."

"Don't you see that you've been *called*—just like I was? You don't think you're here by accident, do you? That our meeting was a coincidence? Ever since I nearly hit you with that dishwater two days ago, I've had the feeling that there's a higher purpose to it all.

"I don't know what it is exactly, or how it's going to play out, but I do think it's critical. My only advice for you is to avoid making the same mistake I did. Don't ignore or deny whatever you're here for, because if you do . . . well, there's no telling how the Universe will remind you."

If Roger was right, then I was in trouble. At least that's how it felt in that moment as I walked back to my room and sat down on the oversized chair in the corner. For some reason, every terrible mistake I'd ever made in the area of love and romance was being stirred up, and the idea that this could potentially serve others seemed far-fetched.

Wasn't it enough for me to just learn the lesson so that I could finally attract a partner I could settle down with? Why did I have to share it? Then I'd not only have to open up my life to deep scrutiny, but also expose parts of myself I didn't necessarily want people to see. I had been hiding so well that I often fooled myself. The idea of talking about my past relationships—as well as all the other unhealed parts of my life that were suddenly lifting their heads out of the water of my unconscious mind—was beyond frightening.

I started scanning through my life, wondering where it had all begun. It was too easy to believe that Linda's death initiated everything that led to my being abandoned on Roger's doorstep. When I was honest with myself, I knew that it went back much further, so far that I couldn't remember a time when I was comfortable being intimate with a woman. Linda was my first relationship, and that didn't happen until my early twenties. I continued reminiscing until a particular time in my life appeared as if from nowhere. . . .

The year was 1995—the year I wrote my first book, *Emissary of Light*. Thirty-three years old, I was suddenly no longer the nerdy guy who had a hard time attracting women. I went from being ignored to being desired; and as strange as it now seems, the shift was difficult to adjust to. I often took advantage of the attention I received and, in doing so, established a bad reputation. I was traveling from city to city promoting books and movies, and it wasn't uncommon for me to leave behind a series of hopeful romantic prospects. Deep down, no matter how it seemed, it wasn't what I wanted, but it wasn't until I met Elizabeth that I was stopped in my tracks.

I moved to Ashland in 2001 and met a woman who was eleven years younger than I was, and instantly fell in love. Elizabeth was an aspiring writer whose talent far exceeded my own, and I was immediately drawn to her. She was beautiful and had a laugh that made my heart race whenever I heard it. Most of all, she became my best friend, someone who seemed to understand and accept me even with all my deficiencies, and I soon realized that I wanted to build my life around hers. It was four years before Linda's death, and although my deepest wish was to rekindle the love I still felt for my former wife, that didn't seem possible at the time. It wasn't what Linda wanted. Elizabeth, on the other hand, was present and real—something I hadn't known for a very long time. I decided to lay everything else aside and pursue love again.

To this day, I don't know what happened between us. It was while we were shooting a film called *Indigo* that Elizabeth ended the relationship. No explanation was given, and her decision to leave Oregon and not have any contact with me sent shock waves through my entire life. A year later, I was still feeling the effects of the loss, so acutely that I had to do something about it or go insane. The fact that I didn't have what felt like real closure was the precipitating factor, and since I suddenly seemed to be in the movie business, I decided to write a script that would give me a creative outlet. The movie *Into Me See* was originally written as a psychological exercise to give me the healing I needed, but when it was finished and I let several friends read it, they encouraged me to make it my next project. The money was quickly raised, and the actors were hired. I was producing another film before I realized it.

When it was released, I was amazed by the effect it was having on almost everyone who saw it. At least one person in every audience broke down in the middle of the film and had to leave. It was hard to take until I figured out what was really happening. People were moved on a deep level—the movie touched a place in the collective consciousness so wounded and unresolved that it had to find expression somewhere. We've all been dumped; and most of us, at one time or another, have also been the ones doing the dumping. Regardless of where we are in our lives or if we're in a relationship or not, those feelings don't just disappear; and for some reason, this little film was helping people get in touch with and release the weight they had been carrying around for years.

I suddenly understood what Roger was trying to tell me. Making that movie was a way of using my experience to help others. It was a strange kind of service, but it was real and genuine; I couldn't deny it. Roger had mentioned that when he tried to get away from being a chef, something he was clearly called to do, he began experiencing health challenges; but when he recommitted himself to it, they went away. Was it possible that my experience with Elizabeth, as well as all the other romantic pratfalls I'd endured, was the same type of thing? What would happen if I found a way to repay my offenses by doing something that would offer other people healing, just like I had done with *Into Me See*?

I noticed a pad of paper on the dresser on the other side of the room and picked it up. There was a pen in my bag, somewhere near the bottom, so I felt around till I found it. Then I sat back down and opened my heart. What did I want to say? If I had only one chance to express how I've hurt the women in my life over the years, what would I write? It was a feeble, even naïve, way to begin, but I didn't feel like I had a choice. All I had was that moment, and the timing seemed perfect. So I started to write. . . .

Sister, Forgive Me

I wish I could have been more conscious when my fears began to rise—
I didn't mean to project them onto you and force you away from me.
I wish I could have held still for a moment instead of running or
forcing you to run—
No matter how far I went, you were still with me, and I was still alone.

There are so many things I've learned from you, so many lessons I've gained—
But most of them were never seen by anyone because I was afraid
to be that vulnerable.
Being alone felt safe, even though I missed what we could have been together—
And melting into another person felt like I was losing something
instead of receiving more.

I wish I could have seen you as my sister—
Instead of a person I could use, then throw away.
I would never have done that to someone in my own family—
Something I feel whenever I think of you.

Sister, I'm sorry I took you for granted and looked the other way—
Didn't honor you, hoped for something more.
I'm sorry I was so impatient, uncaring—
Leaving you to wonder what you did wrong.

You didn't do anything wrong—
And when I'm honest, neither did I.
All those things have brought me to this moment—
And it's a moment I treasure more than any other.

This is when I can look you in the eyes and say I'm sorry,
And in doing so, forgive myself.
I didn't run from you—
It was me I was trying to keep my distance from.

I understand that now, and I can also understand you—
Who you really are!
You are a gift that helps me remember that life is meant to be shared—
And I commit myself to that now.

More than anything, I want you to know that I love you—
Not for who I thought you were or what I could get from you—
But for who you really are.
Now that I see that so clearly, I know I can never forget.

I set the pen down and read what I had just written. There was a part of me that wanted to experience a different emotion from what I was feeling—to be sad or even cry—but that wasn't what I was sensing at all. Instead, my heart felt full . . . I felt relief, like I had just released something I had been holding on to for a very long time. It didn't come from a place of guilt, but from my own resolve to grow and live in a new way.

Everything that had happened with Michele, Linda, Nancy, and Elizabeth had nothing to do with what I'd originally thought. Rather, it was my soul's desire to experience love by releasing the fear I had bottled up inside myself for so many years. It wasn't an end, but a beginning, and I knew that something had just been born.

I sat back in the chair and took a long, deep breath.

CHAPTER SEVEN

A Sip of Wine

I woke up and realized the day had come. I would be flying back to Oregon in a few hours, which meant that my time with Roger was ending. I somehow didn't feel ready for that to happen. The stool in the kitchen felt like it belonged to me, and the idea of going back to a life where food was nothing more than something I ordered from a menu was hard to digest. I had never realized how much spirituality could be found in a vegetable, or in an old family recipe handed down from one generation to the next. I may not have learned to be a first-rate chef in three days, but I did have a deeper understanding of who I was . . . and that alone was a great accomplishment.

I wondered if I should show Roger the poem I had written the night before. It was a tiny glimmer of recompense, the down payment on a larger work I would develop on another day. In the end, I decided to keep it to myself—at least for the moment. The idea that this was an act of service to make up for my past oversights was still a bit remote in my mind, but the seed had been planted, and it was enough for now.

⚜

"Do you remember when I told you about my friend Alain Dutournier, the famous chef from Paris?" Roger asked as I sat down on the stool while he prepared breakfast.

"The one who chose fried eggs for his last meal?"

"Yes. I've been thinking about him quite a bit today. There's something else that happened while he was staying at Drew House that I want to tell you about. Keep in mind that he is among the best French chefs on the planet—his three restaurants in Paris are world-renowned.

"I already told you about the local gentleman who'd decided to host a special dinner to raise money for charity and hired Alain to prepare the meal. I don't think I mentioned that people were going to pay five thousand dollars apiece to attend. Obviously, this man had to have the very best for his generous patrons."

"Five thousand dollars? I see what you mean. That's the kind of event you pull out the big guns for."

"Exactly. Alain does not come cheap, either. He also had to fly two members of his staff here because he certainly couldn't do something like that by himself. Oh, I should also tell you that the host has one of the best wine cellars anywhere. He has rarities such as a Château Lafite-Rothschild from 1864 and a 1962 Maison Leroy. He planned to serve some of these wines at this special event. As I mentioned, Alain and his staff stayed here at Drew House. I suppose everyone thought they'd feel more at home in a place that came with its own Frenchman!"

"I'm sure they felt very much at home," I replied, smiling at his joke.

"I think they did. Anyway, at one point I was curious about how much someone like Alain gets paid to travel all the way to Canada from France to cook a single meal. His answer amazed me."

"It was pretty high, wasn't it?"

"Yes and no. Would you believe that he didn't want to be paid any money at all? I mean it. Of course, his staff had to be paid, but when it came to him personally, he had a very different idea. All that Alain wanted was to be able to taste the wines being served."

"You're kidding. That was it?"

"Well, as I said, some of the wines being served that night were extremely rare. Alain knew it could be his only chance to experience them, and to him, it was more important than the money he could receive."

"So he passed up his fee just to taste a few bottles of wine?"

"I'm telling you this because it reveals something very significant. It shows the real meaning of abundance and service. Do you remember when I said that true abundance is how something makes you *feel,* not the actual thing itself? For example, if you have a handful of money, it isn't the feel of the paper that gets you excited; it's the feeling of what you can buy with it. Some people desire things that are rich and extravagant, while others simply want to feel more connected and whole. It's also something that you have to share because the only way to keep feeling it is to give it away."

"I see, but how did Alain tasting the wines serve anyone else?"

"It served others because Alain then put the feeling back into the food he created. I've heard people talk about that night. It was the most amazing meal of their lives. Part of that was because Alain is a great chef, but the bigger part is that he added something extra. He gave of himself."

"And like you said," I added, "the wine he was able to taste and enjoy was more valuable to him than money."

"Too much energy is focused on what has no real value, and we lose track of what really counts. Alain isn't like that. To him, tasting rare wines was more important than the things he could buy with the money he received. I tell you—I've learned so much from that man, and to me, he is a great example of what it means to be spiritual without being pious."

"I would love to meet him sometime," I said.

"Well, if you ever go to Paris, I'll arrange a meeting. I think you would really like each other."

"Why do you say that?"

"Because like him, you're focused on fulfilling your heart's desire, not just the desire of your ego. You're here right now because you wanted to find love with another person, and even though it didn't turn out the way you'd hoped, you're still open to learning and growing. Once again, I think this is a very good sign—one that will serve you well in the future."

"I hope this leads to something meaningful," I said, hoping that Roger was right. "I guess I came here looking for one thing and found another."

"You came here looking for love, and what you found was . . ."

I waited for him to finish his sentence, but he kept looking at me, waiting for *me* to fill in the blank.

"I'm not sure what you want me to say," I finally said.

"*Love!* You found love . . . just in a different form from what you expected. Everything we've discussed about food and life is held together by love. That's the energy you're looking for, and I think you've found it."

"I think I understand what you're saying, but sometimes it doesn't feel that simple."

"But it *is* that simple," he insisted, becoming more and more animated. "Think of it this way: you cannot find anything that isn't already within you. Right?"

I looked at Roger, confused. "But if you're looking for something, then it can't already be there."

"*Wrong!* This is what most people believe, but it isn't true. If something weren't already inside you, in one form or another, then you wouldn't recognize it when it finally came into view. It could be right there in front of you, and you wouldn't know what it is. Do you understand what I am saying? The love you're looking for is already there. You just need to recognize it."

"That sounds very esoteric. It feels like love gave me the slip and drove back to Toronto. On the other hand, if it wasn't for that, other things wouldn't have happened. Is that what you mean?"

"Consider this," Roger said, smiling. "If I have an olive, or a whole tub of olives, the juice is already inside. Yes?"

"I can agree to that."

"But that juice cannot be enjoyed until it is *ex-pressed,* or pressed out. Do you understand yet?"

"By *expressed,* you mean that it's the expression of what is within it already."

"Now you're getting it! Remember what I said about the garlic? It has to be smashed before it can release its juice. Otherwise, it heals itself and retains the very thing that could bring enormous joy to others. The same is true for you. You've been smashed by Michele. Right? She squashed you, which forced you to start looking at the parts of yourself you were afraid to look at before. Then you were able to express, push out, the juice that's within.

"I've seen it clearly, and I think anyone else would agree with me. In these last three days, you've changed dramatically, all because you were willing to go through this amazing alchemical process. It wasn't gentle perhaps, but being smashed never is. Just ask the garlic or the olive! But now that the juice is out, you can use it creatively. That's what I mean when I say that you found love on this journey, just not in the way you thought."

"But things didn't turn out the way I wanted them to," I replied. "I was hoping that my relationship with Michele would deepen. . . ."

"It's very important for you to realize that you have no direct power over outer things. Anything that seems to be outside you is really a consequence or a picture of something that is already within. The idea that you can affect externals directly, like Michele, without first changing your thoughts, would mean that you can think one thing and produce another. I know this is hard to grasp with the rational mind or intellect, but I'm telling you that it's impossible. It's against the true law of the Universe. This one notion lies at the root of all human misery, whether it be sickness or poverty or even death itself—the idea that you can change your life by focusing on the *outer* without shifting the *inner*."

"What do you mean by the 'true law of the Universe'?" I asked.

"The true law of the Universe," Roger replied, "is simply this: what you think in your mind is what you produce in your experience. *As within, so without.* This has been taught for thousands of years, yet some people still act as if it's being revealed for the first time. The fact is that you cannot think one thing and produce another.

"But now here's the tricky part: it's difficult for us to know what we're really thinking about because thought is much more than just the outer, or conscious thinking, process. There are so many different levels of our thought processes that swing through our minds without us even realizing it. But the truth remains that we can't experience something that is not already within us. Once we see it, our inner process is revealed."

"But what if the thing that's revealed isn't something we like?" I asked.

"Then you should be very happy," Roger said as he stood up and threw his arms in the air. "Now you know what was deep inside your mind—the thing you've been manifesting over and over without realizing it—and you can change it into something that will serve you much better. Maybe you've discovered some habitual, unhealthy pattern that has kept you stuck or unable to shift an aspect of your life. Realizing it's there is the first step to getting through it.

"The challenge is that overcoming these subtle habits—the ones in your mind—is much harder than overcoming the habits you have that are of a physical nature. Why? It's because physical habits are easy to see and witness because they're right in front of you. Inner habits, on the other hand, occur on the screen of your consciousness and are constantly moving and shifting. Your actions are immediate, but your thoughts are cloaked. It takes greater vigilance, and greater courage, to notice and then shift them."

"So the fact that I keep experiencing negativity in my romantic relationships is the result of a habit I've formed long ago and continue repeating?" I asked.

"You formed a pattern somewhere deep inside yourself that keeps getting played out, and will continue to do so until you acknowledge it and then change it. Think of it like this: if I have a recipe and one of the ingredients is listed incorrectly (let's say it says to add two cups of lemon juice when it really should be one cup), I'll keep getting the same result until I can figure out exactly where the mistake is. I could make that dish a hundred or a thousand times, and it will always taste off . . . simply because I wrote down the recipe wrong! When I change it and do it right, however, suddenly the dish tastes the way it was meant to, and the old pattern is released."

"I think I understand," I said. "A pattern in the mind is like a recipe you follow. You've decided what should be added and how much. The cake, or whatever it is you're manifesting, isn't going to change until the pattern is changed—in the case of the recipe. Expecting the cake to change without first changing the recipe is impossible."

"Not only is it impossible, but it's insane," Roger added. "I don't mean insane in the clinical way. We're all insane because we want things to be a certain way in our lives, but we're not willing to do what it takes to make it so. And it really isn't a difficult thing once we understand how the true law of the Universe works. When we do, then everything begins to move effortlessly through our lives, and we see what has always been obvious.

"That's what you've been learning: to see what has always been right in front of you. And it takes great courage to do so, which is what I think you have."

"I have to admit something," I said to Roger. "I don't think I can continue living the life I've been living. I'm finally seeing the patterns that have kept me from receiving the love that has always been right in front of me. Some really amazing women have come into my life, and I pushed them away because of the patterns you're talking about. For the first time, I think I deserve to have the love I've been looking for."

I paused and felt like I had exhaled for the first time in months. Everything I had locked tightly inside suddenly erupted and spewed like lava onto the floor . . . and it felt *great*. I had been judging myself harshly for the ways I'd behaved in the past, but I had no idea how to stop. By admitting what I'd been feeling for so long, I knew without a doubt that I could finally begin to change.

"You really are being smashed," Roger remarked, happily. "I love it! Don't you think it's the most fantastic thing that could happen?"

"*Fantastic?* It *is* exhilarating, but it feels pretty scary, too, like I don't know what I'm doing anymore."

"Then why not let that be fine? It's okay to be lost, unsure in which direction to go. I personally believe that it's much more positive than thinking you know something when you really don't. That's how most people live their lives: believing or acting as if they know their life path instead of asking for help when they need it. It sounds to me like you're asking for help. Would you say that this is true?"

"Hell yes! I'm definitely asking . . . I'm practically pleading."

"Then welcome to a new world!" Roger said with a smile. "One where help comes to anyone who needs it. Ask and you shall receive, right? So the question is: what kind of help do you want?"

I thought about it until I realized I had no idea. As unsettling as the realization was, I didn't have the slightest indication what I was asking for, other than some insight on what my next few steps should be.

"I don't know," I replied. "Once again, I don't have a clue."

"Then we'll stick with the most powerful prayer in the world. It's so simple that it can be summed up in just two words: *Help me!* When you've come to the place where there's nothing left to do but throw your arms up and scream those two words, then you're actually in a powerful position. When you realize that you can't do it on your own, then you can finally see that you don't have to.

"When the juice of your life starts to be squeezed out of you, it always gets used in one way or another. Do you think I smash garlic just to smash it? Of course not! I use every bit of it to prepare the best dish I can, and it ends up serving everyone who eats it. It will be the same for you. None of this is in vain—I promise. You're asking all the right questions and showing enough humility to hear the answers. Just stick with that one prayer, and let the rest happen on its own."

"It's already happening," I said. "Do you think I could have imagined getting dumped by a woman and having it lead to meeting someone like you?"

"I wish I met someone like me every time *I* got dumped by a woman," Roger added, laughing.

"No, I'm serious. I want you to know how amazing this is for me. You've taught me about a lot more than just food or French cooking. I have the feeling that you've taught me about *me*. That's not a little thing."

"None of this is little," he replied, becoming serious again. "But at the same time, it all is. The key to life is to treat every event like it's the most important thing in the universe, while also realizing that none of it matters. It's a strange balancing act, but if you can master it, then you'll be my teacher. That would be a really good thing."

Roger and I spent the rest of the morning talking about cooking and life, and by the time the cab pulled up, I felt ready.

As I picked up my bag and started heading out, Roger walked with me. "You'll have to come back when I'm teaching a cooking class," he said. "You've just begun learning about French cuisine, and I want to take you to the next level."

"I have the feeling we're going to see a lot more of each other," I answered, smiling. "I don't know what form it's going to take, but one way or another, this story has just begun."

CHAPTER
EIGHT

Returning Home

Battered but not broken, I made my way back to Oregon and a life that no longer seemed to exist. If it did, then it would have to find me as opposed to my rediscovering it on my own.

I recalled a vacation I had taken to the Bahamas several years earlier and an excursion to a life-abundant reef to scuba dive. I was a rank beginner and hardly knew what I was doing, but the opportunity presented itself, and I didn't hesitate to accept. At one point about a half hour into the dive, a boat sped over us, a few feet above my head, and the force of the current tossed me around violently. I was out of control, rising and falling in the surf. It may have only lasted seconds, but it was enough to incite a panic I had never experienced before—an overwhelming vulnerability that felt endless.

In that moment, I thought I was going to die, but a deep sense of peace also existed . . . the feeling that I was being held, even protected, by a Divine force. As soon as I relaxed and let it take hold, the current ceased and my body corrected its position and brought me back into right alignment. The panic vanished, and I was able to continue the adventure, but I never forgot the feeling of both terror and release, bound together as if they were familiar bed partners.

I remembered that feeling as I began settling back into my old life. The experience at Drew House had left a kind of sacred wound in my side, as if something terrible had been removed. The imaginary scar it created seemed to tingle when I touched it, but in the healthy way that something tingles as it heals.

Everything I'd learned from Roger—even the graceful way he carried himself and the life he had created in Elora—felt like it was needled into my skin like a tattoo. It was now my job to add texture and color to the design, and I prayed for the courage to remain steady if the strength of my resolve was ever tested again.

A fews weeks after my return, I received an unexpected voice mail from Alice, a woman I'd always been attracted to, but had kept at arm's length given the fact that she was married. Years earlier, I shared my feelings with her when we met in Ireland. I admitted that I felt a strong connection, but had no intention of pursuing a deeper one. She told me that she appreciated my honesty as well as my restraint. Our friendship continued, but since we lived in different states, we rarely saw one another.

As I listened to the recording, the sound of Alice's voice was different from what I remembered. Her words seemed hurried, even alarmed, and she asked that I call her right away. There was no way to know why she was reaching out to me, but my intuition told me to not waste any time getting back to her. I dialed the number and was glad when she answered on the second ring.

"I had a feeling you would call back quickly," Alice said when she realized who it was. "I didn't want to seem overanxious, but I really wanted to talk to you."

"Well, here I am," I replied. "What's going on that's so urgent?"

"It's not that there's anything urgent. I just heard that there are a lot of changes going on in your life, and I wanted you to know that the same is true for me."

When I heard those words, I felt something ignite inside me. I'd thought about it often, the possibility that one day Alice would be available and that we might get the chance to explore our connection. I could almost predict what she would say next and held my breath as I waited.

"Bob and I are getting a divorce," she continued. "He's a good man, and there isn't anything bad to say about him. We've just been moving in different directions for some time, and I guess our separating was inevitable."

"Wow, I can't believe it," I said, less than honest. "Was it your choice, or did you decide together?"

"Believe it or not, it was his choice. I don't think I would have changed things, even though I agreed with everything he was feeling. I probably would have held on and tried to make it work. Well, that's not an option anymore. He made the choice for me, and now it's time to move on."

"Where are you, and what have you been doing?"

"I'm all over the place," Alice responded, and I had the feeling she meant it in more than one way. "I've been spending a lot of time in Peru and also Hawaii. I'm going to be in Oregon and was hoping you might want to get together."

I sensed the restraint in her voice, a feeling I'd felt every time we had been together in the past. How many times had I wanted to say more, knowing it was unwise, or forced myself to hold back when everything inside me wanted to jump forward? Was it possible that she was finally in the same place I had been? And if she was, what did that mean? If she and Bob had recently broken up, the last thing she needed was me pushing my own agenda. At the same time, *she called me,* not the other way around, and although I still didn't know what her intentions were, I felt a glimmer of excitement.

"Are you kidding?" I finally replied. "I would love to see you! How long can you stay? When will you be here?"

"Slow down," she laughed, sensing my enthusiasm. "I don't have any plans, so I can stay as long as we both want me to, and as for when I'll be there . . . how about around two?"

"*Today?* I mean . . . two is great," I said, holding my energy in check. "I have an extra bedroom at my house, so you can definitely stay here; and of course, you're welcome to stay the rest of your life if you'd like. . . ."

There was a long pause as I gauged the impact of my joke. Or was it really a line thrown out to see how she might respond, wondering if she would take the opportunity or shoot me down like a clay pigeon? Either way, it was important that I know where I stood, even if it was up in the air.

"That was a joke, right? Of course you know that—"

"Yes, I was kidding, and of course I know where you are and what's going on. I'm just a bit surprised and slightly overwhelmed that you're on the phone right now. How long has it been since we've seen each other?"

"A few years for sure," Alice said. "I've thought of you often, though, wondering where you are and what you're up to. This will give us the chance to catch up and finally be in the same space for once."

"It will for sure," I agreed, feeling safe ground again. "That's what we both need."

I hung up the phone and looked around the house. It was going to take hours to get it into proper order, and even then it would still look like a single man lived here. I went downstairs to the guest bedroom and stripped the sheets, then picked up the odds and ends that were lying about. The kitchen was the next mountain to climb, and it was Everest-like in its need for tidying. Dishes were piled in the sink, and the counters were filled with utensils and electrical devices I hadn't used in weeks. The rush and frantic motion of cleaning took my mind off the things I shouldn't have even been thinking about: all the possibilities of having Alice— a single woman—staying in my home. I tried to keep myself in check, but I couldn't escape the fact that she was about to arrive on my doorstep in a matter of hours.

I walked into the bedroom and looked at the notepad lying on my desk. It was opened to the poem I'd started writing when I was at Drew House, my first stab at exorcising the demons of my past intimacy issues. It had expanded a bit since then, continuing in the same direction, but fleshed out with new ideas and themes. I picked it up and began to read the new lines:

If there's some way to convince you that I've left my cloister—
Or that I've found new ways to draw the curtains on the former routines
That blinded me to your needs, I hope you'll believe me.

If not, then at least I'll have the witness of my own life as proof—
At least I'll have the attention of my own handiwork to remind me of where I've been.
And where I never want to return.

I wish I could say that I did this for you—
Or that I want to repay you for the memories that have been stirred
Now that we've come to such a hopeful and promising vista.

The truth is I did it for me,
Which is what you said I always do.

But there is one element that makes this different:
I also did it for the one to come—
The one who has been waiting for me to throw off the costume that no longer serves,
And enter the new stage where I know she's waiting for me.

I did it for myself, and I did it for her.
I wish there was something more I could offer you,
Other than my desire to see you whole again.

I was buying groceries a short while later when I saw my friend Tara at the co-op. She was a mutual friend of Nancy's and was the one who had called me when Nancy had passed away. Tara had always been a strong advocate for balance in my life, something I now really wanted for myself. She'd been there for me during my many heartbreaks, and her sage-like wisdom was always a welcome addition to the drama of my strange existence.

As she and I were chatting, part of me wondered if I should say anything about Alice coming to visit. I knew exactly what Tara would tell me: that it was far too early for Alice to be open to another man, even if there had been a connection between the two of us in the past. She would say that Alice needed time and maybe someone to just hold her hand during the turmoil. But hand-holding can remain just that—it doesn't need to progress any further . . . at least not for a while. The truth was, I needed a friend to hear me out, and Tara was perfect for the job.

"I guess my first question is, do you really like this woman?" she asked as we sat down at one of the tables outside the co-op. "I don't mean in an immature, 'do you like her' kind of way. I mean, do you think there's enough for something real to develop? One thing I'm certain about is that you really do want someone solid in your life. I know you've struggled since you lost Linda, and maybe it's time to open your heart again, but not in the way you've been doing. Every woman I've heard about seems to be a passing phase or a distraction—not at all what I think you truly desire. So once again, do you think that you and Alice have the makings for something lasting and real?"

It was the exact question I needed to hear. I could feel the impulsive part of me begin to relax and a more rational side of my brain take over. It was easy to fantasize about Alice when she was married and unavailable, but I had no idea if we were right for each other. She was an amazing, beautiful woman, and her spirit was definitely aligned with mine . . . but what about her habits and routines? What would she be like in a year, or ten years, when the newness wore off and reality set in?

An even better question to ask myself was: *How many times had I played the same game with other women, abandoning reason to chase a vision that was neither consistent nor real?* That's what Alice was at the moment: a vision of beauty and grace, not something that could pass the test of time. I needed more substance, and Tara was already helping me see that.

"I don't have any idea," I finally answered. "We've only known each other as friends when there was a distinct wall between us. What will it be like when the wall is no longer there? I have no clue. There can't be anything wrong with exploring the possibility, though."

"Of course not," Tara said. "There's nothing wrong with any of it. I just think it's important to keep your eyes open—and you're notorious for keeping them shut. Then there's the issue of her just coming out of a long marriage. You knew I was going to get to this sooner or later, and I think it's the most significant element.

She might be looking for something to take her mind off what happened, and that may be why she wants to see you.

"You would be the perfect person for her to ingest like a drug and not feel what needs to be felt. I don't think it would be wise to get into anything too early. Why don't you just have a nice time and get to know each other, while keeping a healthy distance . . . especially if she's the one who wants to move forward."

"Now you might be asking too much," I said, almost desperate. "You want me to be the one who—"

"Yes, Jimmy. You need to be the stronger one because she might not have it in her. Think about how you were right after Linda died. Were you capable of thinking logically, or were you so locked in your grief that you couldn't see straight? Alice is going to be the same way, and you would be doing her a great service if you held a straight line, particularly if she can't hold it herself."

"There's something else I should probably tell you," I said to her. "It doesn't really have anything to do with Alice, except indirectly. I guess it has a lot to do with me, though."

"Why am I getting nervous?" Tara asked as she sat back in her chair. "I have the feeling you're about to say something I don't want to hear."

"Nothing like that," I remarked. "At least not really. We were both pretty close to Nancy, and I know that you felt the loss when she died, just as I did."

"Nancy? What does she have to do—"

"Nothing . . . at least not with Alice. But it does play into what I'm feeling right now. I never told you that Nancy and I started building a possible relationship—a connection that could have . . . maybe even should have . . . developed into more. We saw each other in Chicago, and it seemed to come out of nowhere. It was like we were literally pulled together by something neither of us expected or understood."

"When did this happen?" Tara asked, obviously shocked by the news.

"It was about six months before she died," I continued. "And it was only about a year after Linda died. I had no intention of starting something with Nancy when I saw her, but it was so strong. I didn't feel like I had a choice."

"Why didn't I know about this?"

"I kept it a secret, I guess. I was so afraid, especially when I learned about the cancer. She didn't want to follow her doctor's advice—she was determined to pursue only holistic treatments— and I felt this fear rise in me when I realized the position I was putting myself in. What if she and I went deeper, and I lost her like I did Linda? I felt so selfish, but no matter how hard I tried, I couldn't seem to get to the other side."

"So you didn't do anything," Tara replied as if the pieces suddenly fell into place. "You were afraid of losing someone you loved, something you had just gone through, and then you felt guilty because of what happened."

"I didn't know what else to do," I said. "And I *still* feel guilty. Maybe I could have helped save her life if I didn't step back. Maybe she would still be here today if I—"

"Jimmy, you can't do that to yourself. That was Nancy's choice, not yours. There's no way to know what would have happened, but that doesn't mean you were responsible. I'm more concerned about something else that seems to be the common denominator—the thing I don't think you've looked at until now."

"What do you mean?"

"How many times have you stepped back because you were afraid?" she continued. "You stepped back from Linda when you were young because you were afraid. You've stepped back from many other women for the same reason. I think the emotions you felt were genuine, especially considering everything you had been through a year earlier. But this isn't about Nancy or Linda or any other woman. It's about you: your fear of stepping into the love that could set you free from fear."

I sat there for a moment to let the words sink in. Tara was right, or course. I had been stepping back from so many things, especially from the women who could have helped me work through the fear that had dominated my life for so long. There were so many others. Their faces rose in my mind like phantoms hiding in the back of my consciousness. I had pushed them all away because I was too afraid to let them into my heart and take the risk of being hurt, disappointed, or even completely destroyed.

"And now Alice is showing up in your life," Tara continued, "and there's a part of you that wants to rush in and claim her, just like you wanted to claim all those other women, before becoming afraid and running away in fear. There's something that needs to happen first, the one thing you have to claim before you can really let any of them in."

"What is it?" I asked in a sheepish voice.

"*Yourself.* You need to finally claim you, the one person you've been running from your entire life. It doesn't matter who it is: Linda, Nancy, or any other woman. You're not going to be able to let any of them in until you let yourself in. Does that make any sense to you?"

It made more sense than I was able to say. In a few short moments, Tara dove to the very heart of my greatest issue, the thing that had kept me at arm's length from everything and everyone I wanted to embrace. I hadn't been able to embrace them because I wasn't able to fully embrace myself. Why would Alice be any different? I was about to repeat the same pattern I had been replicating for decades, all because I had never been able to fall in love with the one person I was closest to—*me*.

"Yes, it makes perfect sense," I replied. "To be honest, everything you just said scares the hell out of me. That means it must be true."

"It's time to feel that fear—to feel it and wrap your arms around it. You need to feel the terror you've been hiding from and not run away. It's the only way you'll ever be able to move past it."

I could feel my body growing warmer and sweat began to form on my brow. "How do I do that?" I asked.

"You don't have to do it," Tara said. "You just have to let the fear come and not do anything but welcome it. Think of it like a frightened child. The child doesn't need anything but to be held and loved . . . then the fear dissolves on its own. Do you think you're ready to do that?"

I didn't know how to answer. All I knew was that she was right. I took a deep breath and closed my eyes, praying that I was finally ready.

I was sitting near the window when a red Mini Cooper pulled into the driveway. I stood up, straightened my shirt, and walked to the door. The first thing I noticed when I saw Alice was that she had let her hair go back to its natural brown color, and I immediately liked it. I'd always known her as a blonde, but there was something fitting to this shift. I decided that she'd probably made the change recently—a kind of statement about her new, or perhaps old, life. I went outside and stood on the front porch as she turned off the ignition and opened the door.

"You changed your hair," I said. " I really like it."

"I did it about two years ago," Alice replied, destroying my idea. "I got tired of being a blonde."

By then she was on the porch, and I wrapped my arms around her. Her body felt amazing pressed against my own, and I instantly remembered all the reasons I had been drawn to her in the past. Her slender form seemed to fit perfectly into mine, and the smell of her soft hair set my senses afire. She pulled back and looked at me, and I thought I would get lost in her eyes if we didn't step into the house soon. I suddenly wished that Tara was there to help me remember what we'd talked about. Her advice was slipping into the compost bin in the back of my mind faster than humanly possible.

"You look beautiful," I finally said to her. "Come inside—it's cold and wet out here."

We stepped through the door and took off our shoes. The moment felt so ordinary, nothing like the anticipation and nervousness that had been building inside me. We were normal, and the moment was normal. There was actually nothing abnormal or fantastic about it—well, until she looked at me again and smiled, and just as quickly as it came, my resolve disappeared. I felt my heart jump in my chest as if kicked by an unseen force, and as I turned away to lead her up the stairs to the living room, I rolled my eyes in despair.

"I can't believe it's been so long since we've seen each other," I said. "Now that you're here, it feels like weeks or maybe months . . . definitely not years."

We were in the living room by then, and I motioned for her to sit down on the brown leather couch.

"I know what you mean," Alice said. "That's the thing about people who are so connected on a soul level—years can go by, but it feels like we're always together. I guess that's why I called yesterday. I knew I'd be coming through Ashland and that we needed to see each other. The fact that we haven't been together for so long didn't even enter my mind. It's just what I wanted . . . and here I am."

"And here you are," I replied, not knowing how else to respond. "Why did you think we needed to see each other?"

My words had come out far too quickly; I would have censored myself if I'd known what I was about to say. They were too on the nose, too obvious to have been spoken out loud. I was surprised that she didn't flinch. Instead, she returned my question with one of her own.

"Do you think it's strange I would want to see you right after breaking up with my husband?" Alice asked. "I thought you probably would, but it was worth the risk. I was afraid you would think I was here because of those talks we had years ago, about how things might have been if I weren't married. It felt so normal to talk about it then because we knew it was impossible. It was a game or a fantasy that neither one of us could do anything about.

"I have to admit that I was worried you would think I was coming here to explore things now that I'm in a different position. Obviously, you aren't the kind of person who would want to be with someone fresh out of something so intense. There are a lot of men who would try to take advantage of the situation, but I didn't think you were one of them."

I held my breath as she said those words. She had turned things around so expertly that it was impossible for me to do anything but agree with her.

"I appreciate that," I said. "Yeah, you're right. I'm not that kind of man, so we can both relax."

"That means we can get down to where we were before—the last time we were together. Do you remember?"

I thought back, hoping something would come to mind. The last thing I wanted was to come up short on such a critical question. Something had happened or some words had been spoken that were important for me to recall, but for the life of me, I didn't know what they were. I remembered her passing through Ashland with some friends, and we went for a walk in Lithia Park. It was right after her first trip to Peru, and she told me about the work she was doing with shamans in the Amazon. It was all very interesting, but I couldn't remember if there was a lingering question mark or a commitment we made that I had completely forgotten about.

"This has something to do with Peru," I said, stabbing in the dark. "We talked about going there together sometime?"

"We did? I don't remember that."

"Of course we did," I alleged, hoping I could find a way to make it seem like a real conversation. "You told me about the shamans you worked with there and how it changed your life. We talked about going at some point, and that you would introduce me."

"Okay," she said, playing along. "But that isn't what I was referring to. I was talking about the idea we had about working on a book together. You said that you wanted someone to inspire you, and that we should find something we're both interested in exploring. Then, ultimately, we'd start writing together. Don't you remember that?"

"Oh, sure I do," I replied, uncommitted. "No, actually, I don't remember that at all . . . but it doesn't matter. It sounds like a pretty interesting idea. I just hope I didn't say that to impress you or to pull you into my web."

"As if you would ever do something like that. No, I'm serious! I'd love to do something creative right now. It would help get my mind off everything I've been dealing with. I've been so focused on selling houses and assets, working with lawyers—I need to forget that stuff for a moment. That's why I came . . . to see what the possibilities were."

Alice had completely taken me by surprise. If we did have that discussion back then—and I had no reason to believe we didn't—it was definitely motivated by self-interest. It was wrong of me to say it then, but it would be wrong to discard it now. I had no choice except to see where it all might lead.

"Well, to tell you the truth, there is something going on in Toronto for me," I said. "I was there a little while ago and met this amazing French chef named Roger. He's pretty famous in Canada, but at the same time, he's much more than your typical foodie. He's like a guru. When you sit with him in his kitchen, there are two things he can't help but do: teach you how to cook and talk to you about God and spirituality. I ended up there kind of by accident, but it was just what I needed. I'm going to return in about a week to learn more."

"That sounds really interesting. Do you know how to cook?"

"I don't know a thing about cooking! Especially not French cooking. I've learned a little bit from Roger, but mainly, it's been something else. I don't know if I can really explain it, but he has this amazing way of relating food to life. For Roger, food is the most spiritual thing in the world. Next week, he's conducting a cooking class at the B&B he owns with his wife, Kathleen. Maybe you should come with me. It might be fun to be spontaneous and go on an adventure together."

"You want me to come to Toronto and learn how to cook French cuisine?" she asked in a way that didn't reveal whether or not she was serious. "Are you kidding?! I'd love to go! That's what I'm talking about—the two of us doing something completely outside the box . . . something neither of us has ever done before."

"But I *have* been there," I remarked, "though under strange circumstances. I went with a woman I was seeing at the time, and then she stranded me in the middle of nowhere."

"I thought you said it's in Toronto. How were you stranded in the middle of nowhere?"

"Not in Toronto, but nearby. It's about an hour or so from the city, and it really is in the middle of nowhere. Actually, I think the town is one of the most charming places I've ever visited."

"What's it like?" Alice asked, smiling.

"I think you're going to have to find out for yourself. I love this idea! I was excited to go back, but now I'm *really* looking forward to it. I can only imagine what awaits us. . . ."

Alice in Wonderland

A week later, Roger and Kathleen picked Alice and me up at Toronto's Pearson International Airport. It hadn't been two months since we'd first met, but it felt more like I was returning to visit dear friends than people I had only recently become acquainted with.

Alice was thrilled by the whole idea—the chance to temporarily leave the pressures of her shifting life and learn about the spirituality of food. I tried to explain that it was more than what she could imagine, but my description always fell short. In the back of my mind, I was hoping I wouldn't repeat my last experience with a woman at Drew House. I didn't want to compromise the opportunity we had or to destroy her view of me as the gallant gentleman. It was something I could barely live up to, but I was starting to like the fact that she thought of me in that way.

"You're coming at a wonderful time," Kathleen remarked as we pulled onto the highway. "Elora is amazing during the Christmas season. There are parties almost every night, and the Elora Festival Singers are performing Handel's *Messiah,* which is something you won't want to miss. They were just nominated for a Grammy, you know."

"How could they know such a thing?" Roger interrupted. "It's such a little town—"

"With an amazing choir," she added. "Anyway, we've also had a lot of snow, which means it's like a winter wonderland—not at all like it was the last time you were here, James."

"It was beautiful the last time I was here," I remarked.

"It's always beautiful," Roger said, smiling, "even when it isn't. No matter how it appears, it's lovely . . . even when it's dark and gray, almost like—"

"Honey, they just landed. They don't need you to begin so soon."

"What do you mean? Begin what? This is how I talk to everyone."

"Yes, I know. Trust me . . . I know that very well. I just thought they might like to get some rest."

"Actually, I'm fine," Alice said. "James has been telling me about both of you, and it feels great to experience it for myself."

"Then get ready, because you're going to get your money's worth," Kathleen said emphatically. "In two days we'll be having our December cooking class, which is always an experience when it comes to Roger. People come from all over for his classes."

"I don't know if they come from too far," he added modestly. "For the most part, it's mainly people from the area around Guelph and Elora. Maybe a few come from farther away."

"What will you be teaching?" Alice asked, clearly engaged.

"Lobster bisque," Roger said. "There will be other things, too, but that's the best. Do you cook?"

"I do like to cook," she said, "but I don't know much about French cooking. When James told me about this, I knew I had to be here."

"Like I said," Kathleen added, "you couldn't have come at a better time."

⚜

We soon arrived at Drew House, and after dropping off our bags, Alice and I joined Roger for some cheese and wine in the dining room.

"I hope you like wine," I said to Alice as we walked down the stairs. "You'll be getting a lot of it here, especially Canadian wine."

"Canadian wine? I didn't know that they made—"

"Don't say anything like that around here," I told her. "They're pretty sensitive about that kind of thing in Canada."

Roger was waiting for us with a plate of fine cheese and, of course, an open bottle of wine.

"I don't know how much James told you about our little place, or about his last visit. . . ." He looked at me as he spoke those last few words, trying to gauge what he should and shouldn't say.

"He didn't tell me too much," Alice answered. "Only that food is a very spiritual experience for you. I agree wholeheartedly. It's one of the reasons I wanted to come."

"It is more than spiritual," Roger said. "It's *sacred*. For me, everything is sacred, especially when it comes from the earth. It's the way I was raised in Basque Country. When you live closely with nature, you realize that it is the greatest teacher. Everything you need is right there in front of you . . . you only need to be awake to see it."

We sat down at a table, and Roger poured us a glass of wine.

"That must have been a very good life," Alice said.

"That's an interesting thing to say," he answered. "What is the 'good life'? For many people, it means having five bathrooms in their house. Who needs that? If that's what it takes to have a good life, then you can keep it.

"When I was a young man at my grandmother's home in France, we would fill a bucket at the spring and put it on the stove, then we would wash our feet, first the women then the men. By the time it got to me, it was really bad, but no one seemed to mind. Once a week you got to bathe in water after three others bathed in it first. Most people today will hear that story and say that it's the *opposite* of the good life. Not me! It was one of the best times of my life.

"There is something about simple living that is so much richer than having everything you could ever want. When you have everything, you take it for granted. When you have very little, however, you appreciate everything. Gratitude is a big part of truly living the good life."

"I remember my own grandmother," I said, smiling. "It sounds very similar to her lifestyle. Even when I was a kid, we had to go outside to the pump if we wanted water, and to the outhouse if we needed to use the bathroom. I loved that old house and even thought about buying it after she died."

"My parents and your grandmother had to be very thrifty because they went through a world war," Roger continued. "Food was precious—they would never leave something on the plate uneaten. The First World War was such a stupid war, and the second one was even worse, but it did teach people how to get by. Then after the second war was over, there was the Marshall Plan, which led to the rebuilding of Germany and Japan, something unheard of up to that point. We didn't let Germany or Japan just sink—we lifted them up. If we had done so with Germany after the first war, there wouldn't have been a second. It took a little while, but after a decade or so, Germany and Japan became very prosperous. They were able to move into a whole new way of being, and now they're two of the most abundant countries in the world."

"Where do you see things going now?" Alice asked. "In other words, how do we get to the point you're talking about?"

"You get there by changing from the bottom up. Now, I don't have much faith in things such as the 2012 prophecies, but you never know. One thing for sure is that if something like that happens—an enormous shift that alters our entire society—it will force us to rethink what the good life is. Everything changes. The earth changes all the time! What is meant to happen will happen, but it's not the end of the line.

"This may sound like a contradiction, but I want to do whatever I can to change things. At the same time, I know it's also important to be grateful for things just the way they are."

"Even if they're not so bright at the moment?" I asked.

"Exactly. That's what I was trying to say in the car. It's perfect even when it doesn't seem perfect. No matter what, everything pushes us into balance—both individually and collectively. And that's where food comes in.

"As long as we eat healthy food that's good for us, it brings us into balance. When we eat food that has no value whatsoever, then we're heading for a catastrophe. For me, this is why it all comes down to how we think, and the food we put in our mouths. Keep the focus simple, and the answer is simple. At least that's what I believe."

As he said this, Roger looked at me, the kind of look that says, "I hope you're going to keep things simple this time around." I wanted to say something to let him know that he didn't have to worry about finding me on the driveway the next morning. Whatever was happening with Alice, we were off to a very good start.

"I believe it as well," Alice spoke up as she took a sip of wine. "This cheese is amazing, by the way!"

"You know, here in Ontario, it's unlawful to make raw cheese, but it's okay to sell it," Roger said, as he cut a slice and put it in his mouth from the knife. "The funny thing is that it's fine to make it in Quebec, and then they ship it here. Why do they want to pull the life and vitality out of the cheese just because they're afraid of a little bacteria? It makes no sense. That's what pasteurizing does. They tried to do the same thing to wine, but the taste was terrible—no one wanted it."

"What would the spiritual equivalent be to that idea?" I asked.

"Let me think about that for a moment," Roger replied, then took another slice of cheese. "We allow ourselves to be distracted by everything around us, and that robs us of our vitality. It is what fear does to us. We think we're protecting ourselves, but in reality, we're making our lives so much harder. In terms of food, we've become accustomed to ingredients that have no vitality, or those that even steal our own life force. We don't think so much about food that's alive—we want it fast and cheap. But if we knew the result of it all, especially in our bodies, then we would think differently about it.

"I don't want fast and cheap. I prefer slow, and I'll also pay a little bit more for the best. Maybe I'm the one who's crazy, but it's how I was taught when I was small. That's what you're going to learn while you're here—slow and healthy. Stick with that and the rest will work out fine."

"Slow works for me," Alice noted, as she looked across the table to where I was sitting. "I'm at a place right now where slowing down has been a blessing. Things have been moving too fast, and I think I really needed this trip."

"Alice is going through a divorce," I told Roger, then immediately turned back to Alice. "Oh, I hope you don't mind that I said something about it."

"Of course not. It's not a secret. In fact, everything you've been saying really applies to my situation, Roger. There was so much fear in my marriage, which drained its vitality. Then it started to spin wildly, and before I knew it, I was thrown off like I was on an out-of-control carousel. Sometimes the best thing to do is just hold still, and that's what I'm hoping to do while I'm here."

"Holding still and going slow is a deep spiritual lesson," Roger said. "It's also a great way to cook. . . ."

The next morning I asked Alice if she wanted to take a short walk before breakfast. The sun was shining and a fresh layer of snow had fallen overnight, making the town look even more magical. The crisp air seemed to penetrate my consciousness, and I felt more alive than I could remember. I had come to a crossroad, but hadn't realized it until Michele had gotten into her car and left me standing there in the driveway looking lost and scared.

Now Alice was with me, walking down the sidewalk without the drama and confusion I'd experienced before. This, most of all, was the difference: neither of us felt the need to be anything other than present with what was happening in the moment. I didn't feel the need to try to control our time together; rather, I was glad to let it rest wherever it wanted to be from one moment to the next. I was happy to have Alice with me, and that was enough.

"You were so right about this place," she remarked as we walked. "It's beautiful, especially with the snow and the bright sun. I feel like I'm in Europe somewhere. . . ."

"I felt the same way when I first saw it," I replied. "I didn't know anything about Elora before Michele brought me here. I think it's a pretty popular escape for people from Toronto, but that's usually in the summer, not now."

"It's a good escape for us," she said, as she reached out and took my hand. "You know, I just wanted to thank you for being so patient with me this last week. Everything is upside down right now, and you've been really respectful of my situation. It makes me trust you, and that's something I really need right now."

I was almost shocked by the feeling of Alice's hand against my own. It was something I wanted, something I hoped would happen

. . . but something was stopping me from moving forward. The thought occurred to me that I was becoming a different person, and that it all began with me sitting on the stool in Roger's kitchen, listening to him talk about how to make the perfect cup of coffee. I wanted it to continue, to deepen, and the fact that Alice was there felt like the perfect gift.

"I'm so glad you feel that way." I gently lifted her hand to my lips and kissed it. "I have to admit something. At first, I wasn't sure if I would be able to keep my hands off you. There's this old pattern I have: swooping in to claim what I want, and nothing stops me once I make up my mind.

"Michele told me that when we first met, I overwhelmed her with all the attention. I pulled every trick I knew to get her to fall for me. It's something I've done dozens of times. It wasn't conscious; it's just something I feel and do whenever I meet a woman I'm attracted to."

"How is this different?"

"It's different because I'm relaxed—we're relaxed. I'm not trying to push anything or force you to do anything. I guess I'm more concerned about you than I am about myself, and that's making all the difference."

"What a beautiful gift . . . for both of us," Alice replied softly. "Do you see that it's a gift for you, just as much as it is for me?"

"I do, and it's pretty amazing. The other energy is like a drug, and I thought I needed the rush. Now I see that I don't, and it feels so much better to relax and let things happen."

"You do realize, of course, that if anything is to develop between us, it will come from that place? I can't say what will or what won't happen, but something is bound to come from building trust and being aware of all the patterns that have kept us locked in fear. It sounds like that's what you've been doing, and I have a feeling that Roger has played a big part in that."

"More than I can say," I explained. "To tell you the truth, I'm having fun sharing him with you. He's a really interesting person, isn't he?"

"He's a lot more than interesting. He's *real,* and that's something you just don't see very often anymore. Maybe that's what's happening to you. You're becoming real in a new way. That's how it seems to me, anyway."

"I hope you're right," I told her, smiling. "I *really* hope you're right."

❧

I wondered if I'd really meant the words I'd spoken to Alice. As we walked back for breakfast, I had a strange feeling that I was falling into my old routine, and that my gallant behavior was just a subtle ploy—a trick she wouldn't see coming until it was too late. I hadn't even seen it myself until now, at least not consciously. Did I really want to be the sensitive, insightful man she believed I was? What if I was fooling myself and simply hiding the real motivation: to appear one way only to pursue from another direction? Was I really that creative and loathsome? I hoped I wasn't.

"Bonjour," Roger said, smiling, as we entered the dining room. Three other couples were already eating breakfast, and he was bringing a fresh pot of coffee to replace one that was empty.

"Sit anywhere you'd like, and I'll bring you a fruit salad to begin. Would you like coffee or tea?"

"Coffee for me," I said.

"The same," Alice followed.

"Good. And what about your eggs? James, I know you like yours over easy. How about you, Alice?"

"I'll have mine scrambled."

"Wonderful. Please relax, and we'll talk after everyone has been fed."

Twenty minutes later, the other guests had left the dining room, and Roger joined us at our table with a fresh cup of coffee.

"I have a question I'd like to ask you," Alice said. "Last night, you talked about things being perfect even when they're not. That's a fascinating idea—one I haven't heard before. Can you explain it more?"

"For me, there are two ways of looking at perfection," Roger replied. "The first is the human way, and the second is the Divine way. For us humans, something isn't perfect until it's completely free of flaws. Think of a dancer, for example. Someone has decided what a dancer's body should look like and the way in which she should move. Everything appears flawless. The problem is that in order to live up to that idea, the dancer has to torture herself and do all sorts of things that are not healthy for her body. In the end, the one who is the most 'perfect' is also the one who is the least healthy, especially psychologically.

"On the other hand, there is the perfection that God perceives," Roger continued. "I know that in many religions, there is this idea that to be perfect you have to be without mistakes or sins. I don't believe in that because I don't think it's realistic. That may be the Church's view, but it isn't God's. How many stories in the Bible are about Jesus loving the sinner or showing compassion to those no one else wanted? He was able to see *through* a person's behavior to something that's invisible to the eye.

"Jesus gazed into people's souls, which are completely unaffected by all the mistakes they'd made throughout their lifetime. And here's the really amazing thing: by focusing on the soul, Jesus gave those individuals the greatest gift imaginable . . . he was able to amplify the truth that was asleep within them."

Roger was excited by everything he was sharing, and I could feel his energy increase as he wove his way through the elegant lesson. I suddenly realized how much I had missed him, especially in moments like this when he was on fire with one spiritual concept or another. He was building speed, and all I wanted to do was sit back and enjoy.

"Do you understand what I'm saying?" he continued. "Jesus looks past us weak humans and sees only what is beyond change, what transcends even sin itself. In recognizing that, it grows in us, and we are able to live in a new way. And when we start growing as individuals, then society starts to grow as well, all because we begin to look past what seems imperfect and see perfection everywhere. It's so simple, but I promise you that it's the simple lessons that could change the world."

"So you're saying that our souls and personalities are completely separate?" Alice asked.

"No, I can't say they're separate—just independent. Perhaps it's easier to say that the personality needs the soul, but the soul does not always need the personality. That's the part of you that's connected to the Divine and has never been fooled by separation. You only *seem* to be separated from the people you see around you, or even from God. Your soul knows that none of that is true.

"The problem is that we humans have learned to listen more to what the personality tells us and less to our soul. That's because the soul's voice is so much quieter. It doesn't need to scream to make its point. The personality knows that its position is tenuous, so it makes lots of noise and tries to distract us from the real goal.

"The point I'm trying to make is that God is not so easily distracted. Your soul is the most important thing to God, and when you focus your attention there, your personality follows. One other thing is that your soul has all the time in the universe. It's not bound by the same laws the ego and personality are bound by. In other words, your soul is always looking for experiences to evolve and remember the perfection of life."

"That kind of talk would have been blasphemy a few centuries ago," I pointed out. "Even now, a lot of people would take issue. They believe that when you commit a sin, it puts a stain on your soul; and if you get enough of those 'marks,' then you're in deep trouble. It sounds more like grade school—red marks and all."

"Yes, I know," Roger agreed. "Then this 'loving' God throws us into a fiery pit where we burn for eternity. According to that philosophy, there is no escape—not just for a lifetime, but for all of time. If we make a few mistakes on Earth, we're destined to suffer unbelievable, never-ending pain. Does that sound like a loving God? To me, it sounds more like a vengeful, unforgiving God. This is the God most of us were raised with, however, and it's really tricky to question those ideas. We have this thought in the back of our minds that questioning something, even if it makes no sense, is itself a sin. That's how crazy this way of thinking has made us."

"I know so many really intelligent people," I said, "who are afraid to think through the things they were raised to believe when they were children. They might be successful doctors or lawyers—genuinely bright people—who never make it past a second-grade understanding of spirituality. They accept things that are totally illogical because they were told when they were young that they might go to hell if they asked too many questions."

"Look at how the Catholic Church behaved in the Middle Ages," Alice added. "If a scientist—take Galileo, for instance—discovered something that contradicted the Church's beliefs . . . well, he was locked up or killed. The bishops and popes believed that admitting even the slightest error compromised the entire system."

"That's exactly what they believed," Roger remarked, "and still do. Imagine what would happen if the Church claimed that its authority came from heaven, but then changed its stance on something really important. That would undermine its power, which by then had become extremely political. It would create a domino effect that might bring the whole Church down."

"But that is what's happening now," I said, suddenly feeling the urge to stick up for something I was still wrestling with within myself. "It's not my intention to defend the Catholic Church, but in recent decades, there have been a lot of apologies made. Pope John Paul II even publicly said that the Church has been mistaken about lots of things, including Galileo's work. I don't think the new Pope feels that way, but at least one of them did."

"And I'm not trying to condemn the Church," Roger said. "I'm just using it as an example. As for admitting they were wrong—it's one thing to admit it now, and quite another to do so hundreds of years ago, as it was taking place."

"Wait," Alice spoke up. "That was a big one . . . say it again."

"Think of it this way," Roger continued. "It's true that the Pope apologized for some of the ridiculous beliefs or decisions the Church made hundreds of years ago, but it isn't the same. The world has changed since then. The Church doesn't wield as much power as it once did, especially in Europe. Back then, it would have been a catastrophe to admit such a thing. It probably would have led to complete anarchy. Now it just means that they're admitting to something that is very clearly scientific and easily proven. To go against Galileo now would be suicide.

"Imagine a grown person admitting that he or she did something wrong, or even criminal, when they were a child. To admit it as an adult has very little effect, but admitting it when it happened—well, that is a different thing. The Church did everything it could to stop progress or silence progressive thinkers, even burning them alive, and now it sees that it was all a big mistake. Such a move wouldn't have been possible hundreds of years ago. In the end it couldn't stop the inevitable, and people like Martin Luther finally made an impact . . . but it took almost fifteen-hundred years to happen."

"What about the Fundamentalist churches that continue to believe in the story of Adam and Eve?" Alice asked. "There are a lot of people in the world who completely reject obvious scientific truths and hold on to ridiculous beliefs. They still believe that the world was created in seven days, even though we have millions of years of evidence to show the opposite. Those were the same ideas that were prevalent when everyone thought the earth was flat."

"It just goes to show how insane the ego can be," Roger said, "especially when it's afraid. When you're afraid of something, for instance, you'll see monsters under your bed and all sorts of things that don't make any sense. But that doesn't make it true.

"To go back to your original question, Alice, this is the difference between our idea of perfection and God's. God doesn't need to prove anything because He knows there is nothing to be afraid of. We, on the other hand, are afraid to let go of our strange ideas of perfection and flawlessness because the dominoes start to tumble when we do. It's easier to let the old, crazy stories persist, but I also think it's getting to the point where that kind of thinking will be impossible."

I went to my room, which was next door to Alice's. Something Roger had said touched a chord inside me, creating such a strong vibration that I had no choice but to hold still and pay attention. The idea that *God doesn't need to prove anything because there's really nothing to be afraid of* struck me as one of the most profound statements I'd ever heard.

Is that what I'd been doing all this time . . . trying to prove something to every woman I'd ever met because I was afraid of what might happen if I didn't? If they weren't impressed with me, there would be no reason for them to remain interested. There was nothing about the *real* me that was impressive at all, or so I believed. If I was to have any chance of attracting someone to love and who would love me, then I had to be someone else—someone worthy of love.

The instant that thought came into my mind, I felt it ring inside me: *someone worthy of love.* Whoever that person was, it wasn't me. I was the man who had to morph into something else, something a woman would notice and want to possess. The only way that was going to happen was if I changed, becoming an illusion rather than a real, vulnerable, fallible man.

Someone worthy of love. I couldn't shake the idea from my mind. If I looked at it logically, the thought held no weight at all. I was a successful author, a renowned musician, and an award-winning filmmaker. Why would someone like me be unworthy of being loved by a woman? I began to understand what Roger meant when he said that the mind believes all sorts of insane ideas, none of which are true. For one reason or another, I was afraid of seeing myself as God sees me—as holy and worthy of love. If I could only break through to that vision, then the rest would happen on its own.

On the other hand, all those accomplishments were things I had *done.* They didn't necessarily reflect who I *was.* Was my worthiness based on my success and achievements, or was it something deeper? What about those who had achieved very little in terms of success or fame? Weren't they as worthy of love as anyone else?

I picked up the pad of paper with the poem I'd been working on, and began writing down what I felt in that very moment. As I did, the words flowed out of me, as if they were already fully formed and simply needed my hand to set them free.

I'm willing to let go—
Perhaps for the first time in my life,
And fall into your arms without promise or guarantee.

I'm willing to hold still—
Instead of running whenever the pressure inside begins to build
Every time I think you'll leave me first.

I'm willing to look beyond the past—
And be fully present,
Seeing the future in this moment, instead of in a dream.

I am willing to love you, which really means loving myself—
Which really means loving God,
Which really means loving you.

In the end, it all comes back around . . .
Like a circle.

An hour later, I was walking down the hall toward the bathroom when I heard Alice speaking to someone on the phone. She was in her room and the door was shut; and although I didn't want to eavesdrop, I couldn't help but hear her speaking in a gentle voice to someone she obviously cared about. It didn't take long for me to realize that she was speaking to her ex, and the energy I sensed didn't feel distant or restrained. To the contrary, the tenderness in her voice felt oddly familiar, the tone of a loving wife speaking to her spouse, telling him she was there for him even though they were far apart. I stood there hoping to hear something that would tell me what I wanted to know . . . that it was time for him to let go so that they could both begin anew. Those words didn't come—only the soft tones I hoped she would one day share with me. I suddenly felt as if that day would never arrive.

I put on my coat and walked outside. At first I didn't know which direction to take; I just wanted to think and recalibrate my internal compass. It was time to let go of the fantasy I had of this trip turning into a romantic holiday. The part of me that was attached to a particular outcome came rushing forward, and I realized that I was not as open as I thought I was. Alice wasn't free of her past, and for some reason, I was surprised by that. Having been through difficult breakups myself, especially a marriage, I know firsthand how easy it is to remember the connection and try to make it work again. It was clearly happening in the room next to mine, and I certainly wasn't going to stand in the way.

I decided to walk to the Elora Gorge along a trail that led into a wooded forest, and I stood beside a cliff aptly called Lover's Leap. A sign explained that it was named after an Indian princess who had jumped to her death when she learned that her mate had been killed in battle. Interesting thought . . . but I certainly hadn't come that far. There was no reason for me to do anything but be happy for Alice. There was never a promise or even a definite intention I could hold on to or claim. She was explicit about her need to take things slow and not become attached to an outcome. More than anything, I was angry at myself for giving in to the fantasy of Elora being the place I would finally find love. It didn't happen with Michele, and it wasn't going to happen with Alice.

After a few moments, the wind began to cut through my coat, and I decided it was time to return to Drew House. My walk had helped me put my head on straight once and for all.

I walked through the front door and saw Alice sitting at a table. Of course, I didn't want to say anything about what I'd heard upstairs. For one thing, it was none of my business unless she wanted to share it with me; and second, it was wrong of me to have listened in to a private call. She smiled as I walked in and asked me to sit down with her. I took off my coat and felt a sinking sensation in the pit of my stomach as I pulled out the chair. I assumed that this was when I would hear the news—all about her desire to work things out with Bob and save their marriage. I mentally reminded myself to feign support and offer her the best advice I could, no matter what. I was familiar with this feeling, having felt the sting of rejection many times in my life. Unfortunately, this would be no different, except that it would be tainted with a bit more irony than before. At least I wouldn't have to worry about her taking off and leaving me stranded.

"I just got off the phone with Bob," she said to me. "He's really hurting—really feeling things for the first time."

"I'm sure that was hard for you to hear," I replied, hoping she sensed sincerity.

"Yes, it was very difficult. I really love him and care about what's happening. I don't want him to suffer, but at the same time, if that's what he needs to go through, then I'm going to be supportive of that."

"I'm sure you've suffered as well. It must be hard to go through this when you still care for him like you do. I'd understand if you decided to leave early to be with him. It wouldn't mean anything—"

"What do you mean?" Alice's tone quickly changed. "I'm not going back. Just because he's suffering doesn't mean that anything has changed for *me*. I want to be there for him as a friend. I owe him that. But at the same time, I feel very secure with where he and I are at this moment. James, you don't have to worry about me dropping you and taking off—especially since I know your history here."

"Well, it's not . . ." I trailed off, trying to sound more confident than I really was. "Okay, so it did cross my mind. Maybe I'm a bit oversensitive about being chucked to the side right now. I definitely don't want it to become a pattern."

"Nothing has changed between us," Alice said. "And at the same time, I still need to go slow. The pace has been perfect; it's just what I need. The only thing I know for sure is that I really care for you, too; and I'm committed to being in the moment to see where things lead."

That night we accompanied Roger and Kathleen to a Christmas party and were told to be ready for some surprises. The first was the house—owned by their friends Mark and Marnie—which was exquisitely decorated. The second surprise had to do with the interesting conversations we enjoyed with the guests, as well as the hosts themselves. I began to realize just how unique Elora was and how many of the residents possessed a depth not often seen in such a small community.

Kathleen explained that most of their friends were from elsewhere but had moved when they'd fallen in love with the town, the people, and the lifestyle. Aside from the Elora Festival Singers (several of whom were at the party singing carols), Elora is also the home of a renowned summer festival and a wide variety of other musical and cultural events. I immediately felt at home and could tell that Alice shared my feelings.

"That was the first photograph I bought for my wife," Mark mentioned as he walked over to us. We were admiring a limited-edition print of a famous Georgia O'Keeffe photograph, one of dozens of remarkable images lining the walls of the home. "I actually bought it for Marnie on our first date. We were walking down the street, and she saw it in the window of a shop. She loved it so much that I figured it would be really impressive if I bought it for her on the spot."

"Wow! Did it work?" Alice asked him.

"It did, but the person most impressed was me . . . when I saw the price. I figured I'd better marry the woman because I was clearly making an investment."

"It seems to be an investment that has paid off well," I added. "You two seem so happy together, and your home is beautiful."

"I have Marnie to thank for that . . . both the home and the wonderful life. She's quite an amazing woman."

"It seems like an amazing town to live in," Alice remarked. "I'm surprised to find so much in such a small village."

"You're right," Mark agreed. "It's small but potent. That's why we decided to live here, because we were looking for a place that was exciting and charming . . . somewhere we could feel at home, but which wasn't far from the city. For us, it's perfect."

I was beginning to feel the draw myself. Although I'd started off being abandoned on a cold, wet driveway, my situation had dramatically shifted. It had blossomed into one of the most memorable times of my life. I realized that I owed Michele a debt of gratitude for the gift of Elora and Drew House. I even thought of calling her to tell her what had happened since we last spoke, but then decided to enjoy the moment and move on. I still didn't know what would happen with Alice, but I definitely didn't need to complicate things by adding Michele to the mix.

The next morning, Drew House was abuzz with activity. Around twenty people arrived for Roger's cooking class and were greeted with a glass of champagne, as well as a menu outlining the day's lesson. Several men and women I'd met the previous evening were there and greeted me as I walked into the dining room. Kathleen handed me a glass of champagne, then pulled me to the side and whispered in my ear.

"Don't feel like you need to stay for the entire class," she said. "You know Roger—he'll get going with his stories, and everyone will be so engaged. It's the meal at the end you'll want to be here for."

"I'm here as much for the stories as I am for the meal," I replied, grinning. "I've never met anyone like Roger, someone who has such a spiritual relationship with food. I've learned more just hanging out with him in the kitchen than almost any place I can remember."

"He's pretty amazing," Kathleen agreed. "Imagine living with him all the time. I can honestly say that he lives it, and that's the most important thing to me. It's one thing to sound wise, but it's quite another to live it consistently. Not only that, but he is also genuinely humble. I don't think he realizes how amazing he is."

Alice walked in behind me, and Kathleen handed her a glass.

"What are you two talking about?" she asked.

"Nothing really," I replied. "Just how grateful we are to be here."

"Cheers to that," Kathleen said as she lifted her glass. "And now it's time to get back to work. Sit anywhere you like."

The room was arranged with rows of chairs all facing the kitchen. A gas stove with six burners was facing the group, and a mirror was angled above so that everyone had a perfect view of the action. It was clearly something Roger had done many times before, and I had the feeling that a lot of those in attendance were regulars. I looked out the window and noticed that a promised snowstorm was just beginning, and as I looked around, I realized that there was no better place to be than right where I was at that moment.

"Today, you're going to learn to make a few of my favorite recipes," Roger started when everyone was seated. "I can show you how to prepare everything . . . how much of each ingredient to put in and that kind of thing, but what I can't teach you is what is most important—how to add your love to the recipe. It's what makes all the difference, and it's not something that can be printed in a book or even taught in a class like this.

"I'm sure you've all experienced what I'm talking about—it's the thing that makes a dish explode, not only with taste, but also with energy and life. Why do you think you have such fond memories of something your mother cooked when you were a child, or something your grandmother made whenever you visited? It's because they added the love they felt for you into the recipe.

"You might say that your mother made the best lasagna you've ever tasted, but when you look at the actual ingredients, they're no different from what anyone else uses. Remember, it's the love that gives a dish the energy that connects with your heart and soul. Although I can't teach you how to do it, I can talk about how vital it is.

"The first thing I want you to keep in mind is that anyone can easily do what you're going to see me do today," he continued. "Some of you may think I'm a magician, but it's not true. *Nature* is the magician, and I'm just a conscientious worker who feels more like the eternal apprentice. I'm always learning, just as you're learning right now; and if we stay with that attitude, then I think we should all be okay."

"For most of us, that will be easy," a man in the first row added. He looked around, hoping the others would agree with him, as his wife elbowed him in the side to quiet him down.

"That's good!" Roger exclaimed, smiling. "Because the last thing you want to believe is that you've mastered an art, especially the art of cooking. It really applies to everything in life, though, doesn't it? If you stay humble and treat everything like a child who is just beginning to discover things, then you'll advance much faster than if you decide you already understand. Okay, enough of that. I want you all to know how happy I am to see you, especially knowing a storm is on the way. You must all be very hungry, or really interested in French cuisine."

"It's a little of both," Marnie said. It was only then that I noticed that the host of the previous evening's party was also in attendance. She looked at me and smiled, then turned back to Roger.

"I'd like to ask you to do something that I try to remember whenever I begin cooking a meal," he said. "Our society is so obsessed with getting everything that is cheap and easy, and we forget to honor all the people who bring us the ingredients we need, especially the ones that are of the highest quality. I always buy the best I can find because it shows respect not only to the farmers and the grocers, but to my body as well. Don't you think your body knows the difference? Of course it does, and it responds when you treat it lovingly. It's so important to begin with a sense of honor and gratitude, and I promise it will find its way into every dish you prepare."

I sat back and listened to Roger share much of the wisdom he'd shared with me as I sat on the stool in the kitchen when we began our friendship. It was clear that there was no distance between what he taught and who he was. They were, in fact, the very same thing. I watched as the people in the room leaned forward and took notes, clearly captivated, almost hypnotized by what they heard. Then I glanced at Kathleen, who was sitting in the back of the room by the door, beaming with pride. Alice noticed me looking around, and reached over and took my hand.

"I'm so glad I'm here," she whispered. "You're such a gift to me."

I squeezed her hand but didn't say a word. I just smiled and felt the same about everything I was experiencing. Roger went on to demonstrate the proper way to prepare canapés gravlax, which was an appetizer consisting of salmon and asparagus in puff pastry. Then he began the most complicated dish: the bisque de homard, or lobster bisque.

In the saucepan next to him, he passed out samples of the bisque, which he had prepared earlier, so everyone could appreciate the final product. Then Roger shared the recipe for coquille de fruits de mer (seafood shells with chunks of fresh lobster, scallops, cod, and steelhead); and launched into a recipe for roasted chicken with garlic, which ended up being my personal favorite. Garlic, after all, had already played such an important role in everything I learned from Roger.

Just when I thought it couldn't get any better, Roger demonstrated how to prepare roasted sirloin and scalloped potatoes. And he topped it all off with a rich orange cake made from a recipe he'd picked up when living in Australia. Two hours passed by like minutes, and before long everyone was sitting at their designated tables, enjoying the spectacular dishes we'd just watched Roger prepare. I chatted with the others who were at my table, but for the most part, I sat in my chair feeling overwhelmed by my good fortune. I didn't know what I had done to deserve this experience, but I didn't want to let it pass without savoring every moment and bite.

That evening, Alice and I were sitting by the fireplace in her room, talking and drinking a glass of wine. As I sat there, I realized how comfortable I was, not only with her, but also with myself. So much had changed in such a short time . . . more than I would have ever thought possible.

A blanket of calm seemed to have descended upon every part of my life, and it wasn't because of Alice or Roger or anyone else. It was due to something I had released, although I wasn't entirely sure what it was. All I knew was that I felt lighter, as if a heavy weight had been lifted off my back. I sat back and enjoyed the realization, hoping it would continue.

"How do you think this is going?" Alice said, as she tapped me on the arm and pulled me out of my reverie.

The question shocked me, partly because it was so direct, but mostly because I was asking myself the exact same question in my mind.

"Well, I'm really comfortable. I think that says something important. How about you? How would you answer that question?"

"I'm here, aren't I? I'd say it's going pretty well."

"Really?" I asked as I leaned in an inch or so closer to Alice. "You think this is going well?"

"Of course I do . . . as well as it could possibly go. But there's a question I want to ask you, James, and I hope you'll be honest. I want you to think about the time we've shared—the prior week in Oregon and now here at Drew House. Do you think this is something you really want?"

"Are you asking me if I want us to be together?" I instinctively took her hand in my own. "I've given it a lot of thought, and to tell you the truth, the answer seems to be floating somewhere out of reach. Obviously, I'm drawn to you and always have been. At the same time, I sense that there's something else. Maybe it includes a relationship, and maybe it doesn't. I feel like I'm in new territory, because I'm usually not so indecisive."

"I don't think you're being indecisive at all," Alice replied. "I think you're being real . . . and honest." She sat back in her chair and let go of my hand. "And I can relate to what you said. There's a part of me that wants to move forward and another part that needs to hold still. I'm not sure if I'm ready, but the fact is that I want to . . . be ready, that is."

"I think we're ready to be right where we are," I said. "I used to think that it would be simpler than this, and maybe it is. I'm certain that you've somehow opened up a door for me, and I think you've helped heal something in me as well."

"What did I help heal?"

"Returning to Drew House had the potential of throwing me into chaos. The last time I was here, things were a lot more complicated. Coming back, I wasn't sure if I was going to be able to continue my shift."

"Are you talking about Michele?" she asked. "If you are, then I think it's time to let that go. You can let the relationship heal at any moment because it really has nothing to do with her. It has to do with you and your willingness to grow, just like me. Ever since you and Michele parted, you met Roger, and then you and I reconnected. You've also had all sorts of powerful internal realizations. Michele's leaving you here was probably one of the best things that could have happened to you."

"It's not the first time I've considered that possibility," I said, "but this may be the first time I actually feel happy about getting dumped."

"It's the least I could do . . . well, to help you see that."

"You've been a great friend to me," I replied, smiling. "I may need to keep you around for a while."

Two days later, Alice and I landed in San Francisco. She was to meet a friend and begin a new adventure without me, and I would head back to Oregon. We drove into Oakland together and enjoyed a final lunch. We didn't say much as we ate; we just held the space for whatever had been birthed between us since Alice had first called and I had asked her to go to Drew House with me.

I sensed that rather than an ending, this was the start of something neither of us could quite see in the moment. I'd experienced a profound shift, and I acknowledged that I wouldn't have room for anyone else until I let the roots settle deeper. I knew I was standing in front of a door that was opening to a new life, but I also felt as if I were still miles away from where I wanted to be.

CHAPTER TEN

The Heart of the Matter

"There's something I think I need to do," I said to Roger, as I held the phone closely to my ear.

Three weeks had passed since Alice and I had returned from Drew House, and although my life felt more settled than it had in years, something still seemed unfinished . . . as if the final piece of the puzzle was missing. I'd learned to be like garlic and let myself be smashed to the point of no return; I'd allowed myself to release the guilt I felt for what had happened to Linda and Nancy; and I'd even opened my heart in a new way—one that was less concerned with results or making someone feel a certain way, and more focused on honoring the connection and letting God guide every step.

What started off as a troubled beginning had actually blossomed into a fresh lease on life, and I could barely remember what things had felt like beforehand—even being stranded in the driveway at Drew House seemed like it was in the distant past.

The missing piece lingered, however, and it had something to do with Roger. More specifically, it involved a couple of stories he'd mentioned in passing—about a man he knew, the famous chef Alain Dutournier—which hadn't seemed overly significant at the time. The strange thing was that since I'd returned home, I couldn't stop thinking about those stories, as if I needed to find out more or to actually meet the person Roger was clearly very impressed with. *Perhaps that was it!* If Roger thought so highly of Alain, then he had to be special—or, at the very least, he was someone I could potentially learn a few important lessons from.

I called Roger as soon as I woke up the next morning, anxious to share what had come to me the previous evening. Like a seed falling out of my pocket when I wasn't paying attention, it began to sprout roots the instant it hit the ground. As much as I wanted to discard the idea altogether, it was the only thing that brought me a sense of relief and comfort. It was the final puzzle piece, and I needed Roger to help me see it through.

"James? Oh, hello! It's nice to hear from you," Roger replied. "What is it you need to do?"

"Do you remember when you told me about the famous chef who stayed with you at Drew House?"

"Yes, of course. Alain Dutournier. Why are you thinking about him?"

"I don't really know, to tell you the truth, but I can't stop. It was something about the way he answered your question—about having fried eggs for his last meal on Earth."

"Yes, but not just any fried eggs. Remember, his last meal would be one that would stir memories of a very happy time. It was symbolic of his mother making him breakfast and that feeling of love that stayed with him his entire life."

"A feeling that stayed with him his entire life," I repeated. "And you and I talked about the Last Supper on that first day I sat on your kitchen stool. Do you remember? You said that food is both physical and spiritual, and that if we ate with that belief, then every meal would be sacred."

"I said that?" he responded, in a way that almost surprised me. "I can never remember what I say anymore."

"I don't know if those were your exact words, but that's how I recall it. You also said that French people treat food in a sacred manner, especially when they eat together—that is, they cherish the time and don't rush or try to hurry things up."

"Sure, I remember all that," Roger replied.

"Well, that's what I need to do," I said. "I want to go to France and experience what you've been saying firsthand. I feel like I need to learn from Alain, just like you did. My intuition is telling me that he's the final piece of the puzzle that's been taking over my life these past few months . . . as if something might happen there to bring it all together.

"Ever since my time at Drew House, I've gone through a powerful transformation—like the garlic getting smashed—and now that I'm all exposed on the cutting board, I feel like there's one last thing I need to do. I don't know if I'm making sense right now; it's just a strong urge inside me. Going to Paris, somehow, will help me figure it out . . . whatever *it* is."

"You want to eat at Alain's restaurant?" Roger asked. "I'm not sure what that would do, but I can help you meet him, if that's what you'd like."

"Yes, it is! I was hoping you could introduce us, and maybe even set up a meeting so I could talk to him."

"I'm sure I could arrange that for you, but I don't think Alain's command of English is very good. You'll need to get someone to translate."

"Great! I'm certain I can find someone to do that," I replied excitedly. "I think I need to leave right away, too. For some reason, this feels urgent—as if I don't have any time to waste."

"Okay. I'll e-mail Alain today and see if he's in Paris. This is a time when he might leave on holiday, but I can find out for you."

I'd never experienced such a powerful urge before. Luckily, my schedule was open and there didn't seem to be anything holding me back, except for a small voice within that wondered if I were jumping into a pool without knowing if the water was there to break my fall. More than anything else, I wanted to initiate something, to follow a path that would lead me to some kind of completion. Everything I'd been through with Linda—as well as all the other women who had taught me one lesson or another—needed to reach its climax. I knew I wouldn't be able to fully move on in my life until I achieved it in some way.

Later that night I was talking to Alice on the phone and told her my idea, especially about my need for some type of closure. As always, she listened patiently and then paused before answering.

"What's the common thread that pulls everything together?" she asked. "I want you to think way back—not just to Linda, but even farther in the past. Every woman you've encountered—from your mother to talking to me right now—has been holding out some kind of gift for you. What do you think it is?"

"I have no idea," I replied, hoping I could get away from where Alice was steering the conversation. The thought of looking back over so many years felt overwhelming, and I wasn't sure I could do it. "My relationship with my mother seems fine. We've never had any real difficulties or problems, at least not that—"

"What are you doing?" Alice asked as if she could read my mind. "Don't go so fast. You're shooting past the most important woman in your life: your own mother. You don't think there's anything there to look at, to examine more closely?"

"I don't know," I finally said. "No, actually, I don't think there is. I have a good relationship with my mother."

"Do you? Think way back, not just with your mind, but with your heart. I'm not saying you need to find something negative that she did or said to you. But I think you're overlooking something, either because you don't understand how big the impact was or because you're afraid of it."

"I don't think there's anything there," I answered. "If I look back to when I was a really small kid, everything feels pretty normal."

"How old were you when your sister was born?" she asked.

"Well, my brother, Todd, is a year older than I am, and I'm three years older than my sister, Lisa. But what does that have to do with—"

"Just stay with me. Try to go back to when you were three or four. I know it's hard to remember it in detail, but if you really try, some of the emotions might resurface. Imagine being there when your mother came home from the hospital with your baby sister. She was an infant and needed lots of attention. You were a little boy then who needed his mother, but at the same time, your needs could wait a little longer. See if you can go back to that time, and try to feel the emotions you were experiencing."

I closed my eyes and imagined the scene to the best of my ability. I could see my brother who was bigger and more independent than I was, and then I imagined my mom holding Lisa. Of course she was smiling and holding her close, like any woman would do with a newborn. I could see myself sitting on the ground watching my mom, and even though there were toys all around me, I didn't seem to be interested in any of them. My eyes were fixed on what was going on in the big chair in the corner of the room. Swaddled in a blanket, my sister was making faint sounds as she drank from a bottle. My mother glanced over at me, but only for a second. Her eyes went back to my sister so she could be present with her. I sat there hoping she would look back over at me again and smile, or acknowledge me in some way. She didn't.

That's when I felt it. I was jealous! Only a week earlier, *I* had been the one receiving most of the attention. I was the baby, and my mother spent most of her time taking care of *my* needs. I didn't really understand what was happening with all the activity and the fact that her belly was growing larger. None of it mattered—only that I got what I needed, what any three-year-old would need.

Suddenly, the images disappeared, and I felt pulled back into the present. I didn't like what I'd felt at all.

"You're back," Alice noted, sensing the shift. "What are you feeling right now?"

"I'm angry," I replied, as I filled her in on what I had seen. "I don't even want to watch it anymore. I know it's just a memory of something that occurred more than forty years ago, but it still hurts."

"Of course it does. That's because you've had it locked away for so long. It's a pretty hard thing to face—being mad at your mother. You had no way of knowing that she wasn't doing anything wrong, or hurting you on purpose."

"But I was still important," I said as I felt the emotion building inside me. "She didn't have to spend all her time with Lisa and forget all about me."

"There are two things I want you to do now," Alice said in a voice so gentle and soft that I could hardly hear her over the phone. "The first is that I want you to keep feeling whatever it is you're experiencing. Don't push it away. But I also want you to ask yourself a question. I want you, the older you, to ask yourself what was really happening. Had your mother *really* forgotten about you?

"I know that's how it felt at the time, and it may even feel that way now, but is it true? You can look at it from a different perspective if you wish, not from the point of view of a three-year-old but as a mature adult. Was your mother really pushing you away, or was that just how it seemed?"

Of course I knew the answer, but at the same time, I felt deeply confused—the same way I had felt as a small boy. There was no way I could have interpreted what it was or what was really happening at the time, and yet for some reason I had the sense that it was important for me to feel it again—as if I couldn't release it just by thinking about it intellectually, but as a small child. The more I let that emotion fill me, the more I knew that it was time to let it go. I could feel the older me reasserting himself, letting the younger version of me know that everything was going to be okay.

I imagined myself walking over to the younger Jimmy and picking him up, lifting him high in the air. I suddenly had the sensation of being both at the same time: the forty-eight-year-old and the three-year-old. It felt good to be held, and it felt good to hold the little boy I thought I had forgotten. After about a minute, I knew it was time to set him down, and at the same time, I opened my eyes again.

"I have one more question for you," Alice said. "How do you think that feeling—the one you buried inside yourself for forty-five years—has influenced the way you've dealt with women all your life?"

I took a deep breath because I knew I was entering uncharted territory. Was it possible that I'd carried the same emotion into every relationship—the feeling that I wasn't good enough to be held and loved, and that sooner or later my partner would realize her mistake and move on to someone better? Is that why I always did the pushing, because I didn't want to be pushed?

It was easier to play the fool than stand in the fire and allow love to fully transform the sadness still locked tightly inside me. I became aware of a feeling I had never really noticed before in the center of my stomach. It made me feel so alone, so vulnerable, that I didn't even want to go on. It had been resting there just out of view throughout my entire life, and I suddenly felt it as clear as day.

Like Toto pulling open the curtain that had been hiding the humbug wizard, I saw the one who had been pulling the levers and strings of *my* life. He didn't seem that powerful at all—more like a weakened old man who could barely survive on his own. I stared at him and he stared back. For a second, it seemed as if he was going to pull the curtain shut again, but it was too late. I had seen the truth, and there was no way he could play the same role as before.

The little old man picked up a hat that had been sitting a few inches to the side and placed it on his head. Then he looked at me and smiled one last time, before turning and walking away. He walked into a mist and disappeared, and the negative energy in my stomach vanished as well.

"Welcome to a new world," Alice said, sensing my transformation. "How do you feel?"

"A bit scared," I admitted. "Part of me feels great because I've released something so ancient, but at the same time, it feels like something left me—a part of myself that has kept me safe for a long time."

"Of course that's how it feels," she noted. "That's the way it always felt—that it was safer to push away the women in your life before they realized who you really were. None of that was true, though, even though it felt like it was. It was like a friend or an ally, one you had trusted implicitly. But now you've realized you don't need it anymore."

"I don't need it anymore," I repeated. "But now what?"

"Now you celebrate!" Alice exclaimed happily. "I think you've earned a little vacation, and maybe a final meal that will help everything you've learned fall into place. Like Alain's last meal of fried eggs . . . well, yours is going to be quite a bit more lavish than that, all because you deserve it."

"I *deserve* a meal prepared by Alain?" I asked, finally putting together what Alice was saying.

"Not only that, but there's someone else who deserves it as well. In fact, I have a strong feeling you won't be going to Paris alone. . . ."

Alice and I said good-bye, and I spent a few moments being still before throwing myself back into activity. I decided to check my e-mail before booking a flight to Paris and was surprised to see a new message from Roger with the subject "Paris Trip." I immediately opened his note and started reading:

James: Do you want me to go to Paris with you? Kathleen said she can use her air miles to get me there, and if you're willing to pick up the lunch with Alain, I would love to come along. I contacted Alain, and he said that he could meet with us after we dined at his restaurant. So if you want a great French translator, then I'm your man! Let me know, and I'll have Kathleen arrange the flight.

I was amazed by how well everything was falling into place and was suddenly filled with a new energy throughout my entire being. I quickly replied to Roger, telling him that I'd love to share the experience with him and that I couldn't believe how generous he and Kathleen were. It was the perfect answer to my prayer, and there was no way I could turn away from such an amazing opportunity.

Minutes later I was booking my flight to Paris, knowing that in just three days I would be able to follow through on Alice's suggestion. It *was* time to celebrate.

CHAPTER ELEVEN

An American in Paris

A heavy blanket of clouds hovered over the runway, and as my plane descended out of the sky that was more like a thick soup, I had the sense that everything was about to change, as if I were finally coming to the end of a strange and fantastic dream. Dreams, I realized, can be mundane or terrifying, depending, of course, on one's immediate point of view. We usually want the scary ones to end as quickly as possible. That's obvious. What isn't so apparent is that even the good dreams have to reach a climax, for they were never meant to be lifelong companions. The moment comes when the alarm clock goes off and we open our eyes. Then it's time to wake up and get on with it. Real life begins at that moment, whether or not we want it to.

For the most part, my "dream" had been pretty good. I had accomplished most of the things I'd set out to and considered myself a happy person. Unlike the vast majority of people in the world, I had stuck with my "plan A" and had come out pretty much unscathed. But when I was truly honest with myself, especially in the last couple months, I knew that there was a deep ravine inside me that had been hidden from view, but was now visible. I had mistakenly believed that it was a bottomless pit, and that I could fill it with all the mistakes and missteps I'd made over the years.

Then without warning, it was overflowing, and I was forced to deal with the inevitable. There was no more hiding, just as I realized that I was destined to repeat my mistakes in the future as long as I pulled the past into every new relationship. Alice said that this was a time to celebrate everything I had learned, and although it felt strange, I decided she was right.

I got off the plane in Paris and began walking toward baggage claim, and even though I was tired from the long flight, there was a lightness to my step that I couldn't deny.

I had the address of the hotel where I was to meet Roger, and that was all. It was going to be somewhat tricky finding it, but the train ride to Gare du Nord, then the short taxi to the hotel, went off without a hitch. The woman at the front desk gave me a room key and told me that Roger had already checked in. Our room was across a narrow alley and up three flights of stairs—with no elevator. By the time I'd hoisted my suitcase and guitar to our door, I was covered in sweat, but I'd made it. The adventure was about to begin. Just as I was pulling out the key from my pocket, the door opened and Roger appeared before me.

"Bonjour," he said, smiling. Roger's eyes were red, and he rubbed his face with both hands, clearly just waking up from a nap. His flight had arrived earlier that morning, which meant that he had to wait several hours before I got there. When in a similar situation, I do my best to hold off sleeping until bedtime, knowing that even a short nap usually destroys my ability to fall asleep at a normal hour. On the other hand, given the fact that I can rarely sleep on overnight flights, the urge to close my eyes is sometimes just too great. This was clearly the case for Roger.

"We made it!" I said excitedly as I pushed my suitcase through the door. "I can't believe we're in Paris . . . all for a single meal."

"It may be one meal," he replied, "but it's not just *any* meal. I stopped by the restaurant earlier and picked up the menu they'd created for their New Year's Eve dinner. Here, take a look at this."

It was a tiny piece of paper folded in half with writing I couldn't understand.

"I don't know what it says, but it looks impressive."

"Just read this part," he said, pointing toward the bottom where the all-inclusive price was listed. *Four hundred thirty-five euros!* I swallowed hard.

"Wow. That's something like six hundred dollars . . . for one person?!"

"Yes, per person. Now you know the kind of restaurant we're dealing with. It's amazing they can charge those prices . . . but this is Paris, a city that lives for food."

I sat down on the bed and took off my shoes. It felt good to be with Roger again. It was a continent away from Elora, but it felt normal to find him waiting for me in France, as if this was his natural environment. I knew that in many ways it was. He'd lived in Canada since the early sixties and had spent a dozen or so years in Australia and Tasmania, but this was the soil on which he'd been born and bred. It was like coming home to his mother, and the fact that I was getting to share the experience was an amazing gift.

"So what's the plan?" I asked him. "When do we see Alain?"

"Our reservation is for lunch tomorrow," Roger replied. "I figured lunch would be better, as Alain could spend some time with us when we're finished eating. It will also be better for the price, since you're paying. . . ."

"I appreciate that," I told him. "I have the feeling that tomorrow's lunch will be better than any meal I've ever had."

A half hour later, we were walking the streets of Paris. We strolled through the enormous square outside the Louvre, then once we crossed the Seine, we made our way into the trendy Left Bank and passed an assortment of antique shops and art dealers. The clouds were still ominous and gray, but for the moment there was no rain, and we carried on without incident. I found myself relishing every second, hoping that if this was a dream, I wouldn't wake up anytime soon.

Even in the wintertime, under cloudy skies, Paris was magical and vibrant. We walked the city for hours, and Roger showed me where his grandmother had once lived—across from the Eiffel

Tower. In the mid-sixties, she'd sold her apartment for a few thousand dollars, which today would be worth *millions*. Once we were back on the Right Bank, we walked by the Opéra de Paris, an amazing and elegant structure, and then passed countless stores with the word *Soldes,* meaning "sale," posted on their windows. I later learned that January is the month when most stores have big sales to move out their leftover merchandise before bringing in the new items for spring.

By the time evening fell, the streets were overflowing with people, and I had a difficult time telling if they were going anywhere in particular or just enjoying the drama and life of the city.

"When we were at Drew House," I said to Roger as we walked, "you spoke to me about service, especially about finding the thing we most need to heal, and helping others who have the same issue. I don't know exactly how to explain it, but what you said really had an impact on me."

"Yes, I remember," he replied. "If there's something we need to heal, the best way to do so is to help someone else heal the same issue. It's because we can't give something we don't already have, which I think is one of the most mysterious and important laws of the Universe. We usually go around thinking, *I need this and I need that,* but that just keeps the focus on what we don't have. The key is to find the thing we need, and become the source of it for another. Then we realize that the answer was inside us all along."

"I've been experiencing that for myself, but in some really interesting ways. Even though it's a bit embarrassing, I want to share it with you, especially since you've witnessed some of it. I'm starting to realize all the ways I've hurt women over the years by treating them callously or just being insensitive. It really escalated over the last fifteen years or so when I started to do well in my career . . . mainly because for the first time in my life, women were noticing me."

"Is that just because you were becoming well known?" Roger asked. "I'm only wondering because you seem to think that before you were famous, women weren't interested in you. Is that true?"

"I guess so. I was never very cool in high school—in fact, I was a bit of a nerd. It wasn't until much later that it all shifted."

"So you think that the reason you attract women is because of what you do rather than who you are," he replied in a tone that forced me to carefully take in what he was saying. "In other words, who you are when you're just being yourself isn't very attractive. Do you believe that?"

"Do *I* believe that?" I was trying to buy myself time. "I don't know . . . but when I look at it honestly, I guess I do. I never thought of myself as being worthy of deep and lasting love with a woman I really admired. Whenever I was with someone I thought was beautiful or amazing, I pushed her away."

"What about Linda? Didn't you say you thought she was the most beautiful woman you had ever met?"

The question struck me like a lightning bolt. Roger was right. When I first met Linda, I was stunned not only by her beauty but also by her presence—and I never lost that feeling. Was this the real reason I sabotaged our marriage, because deep down I believed that I didn't deserve her? I'd fought for years to get her back, but even if I had, I suddenly realized that I probably would have repeated the same pattern. It was easier to mourn her loss and dream about what might have been rather than heal the underlying cause of my insecurity.

"You want to know about Linda? Well, to tell you the truth, she represented everything I didn't deserve. I guess that's why I lost control and pushed her out of my life. I had this fantasy of her moving to Oregon and seeing how I had changed, but even if she did, the real thing that needed to be healed was still there."

"So you still have to heal the wound that makes you feel like you don't deserve love," Roger replied gently. "How are you going to use that as a way of serving others? Perhaps by helping those who have been injured by someone like you?"

Someone like me! The words stuck in my throat when I tried to swallow. There were millions of men like me in the world who had betrayed or disappointed the women who placed their love and trust in them. Maybe I wasn't there just to heal my own past relationships. . . . Perhaps one man having the courage to stand up and apologize for all the ways in which men have hurt women would be the beginning of something monumental.

"I started working on something," I said. "I'm writing a poem called 'Sister, Forgive Me.' It's about acknowledging what I've done and somehow healing the wounds I've inflicted . . . but it goes beyond that. I thought it represented all men who have been unconscious and neglectful. Maybe by sharing it, it would plant a seed and take root in the consciousness of all of us. Does that make any sense?"

"It makes more sense than you realize," Roger replied as he put his hand on my shoulder. "It's like a homeopathic remedy. It only takes a tiny amount of the very thing that caused the disease to heal it: one person deciding to shift his perception and become the source of healing for others. Tell me more about what you're writing."

"It's still a rough draft, but it feels so good to talk about it. Maybe I'll get it published, or maybe I'll just share it with the women—and even men—who might understand where it comes from."

"And where is that?"

"It comes from my desire to change and heal. My longing to accept the love I've pushed away, thinking I was better off being alone or that I would have an easier life if I didn't feel too much. I don't know what's going to come of it, but I already notice its effects in my own consciousness, and it feels great."

"This is what is very important," Roger pointed out, smiling. "If it helps others, that's wonderful, but this is for you first. What is vital is your willingness to be the source of the healing you need. Hold on to that, and the rest will work out on its own."

By early evening, Roger and I were exhausted after a long day of traveling and exploring the city. The next day would be the grand finale we had been preparing for, and we wanted to be well rested.

I had no idea what Alain would add to everything I'd already learned from Roger, but I couldn't wait for the experience to unfold. The puzzle would finally be complete.

When I woke up the next morning, Roger was sitting on the side of his bed with his eyes closed. He seemed to be deep in meditation, focusing his attention somewhere I couldn't see or follow.

As I watched, I thought back to all the time I'd spent with him, sitting on the stool in his little kitchen sipping coffee or in the dining room drinking wine, talking about food and the nature of life and divinity.

For a second I thought everything that had happened was somehow orchestrated by the place within me that was finally ready to transcend my old life and embrace a new reality I was only beginning to recognize. I felt ready, not only for this final step, but for every step that would follow. The path was obscured by many of the doubts still floating through my mind, but they had grown malleable, no longer hard and unyielding, but soft and pliable like clay.

I reached over and picked up my notepad, the one that contained my poem. The conversation I'd had with Roger the previous day inspired more ideas that I wanted to get down on paper. I knew the best thing I could do was stay out of my head and focus on my heart, letting the deeper impulse within reveal itself.

I took a deep breath and opened the door that led to the dark, solitary cave inside me where I had been hiding for so long. It was time to let the light stream in, and no longer allow shadows to rule my life. . . .

Sister, I admit that I'm not really sure why I'm writing these words.
Are they for you, or for something I need to find within myself?
Perhaps this is even bigger than the two of us,
Something meant to heal the root of our frailty—
Or even all human frailty.

All I know is that you didn't deserve the way I treated you.
There, I said it!
You never deserved the many ways I lied, even when I told you the truth—
Or the ways I hid, even when I seemed to be right in front of you.

Here's what you did deserve:
The open, honest me I'm just beginning to discover.
I wish I could have been more in touch with that person when we were together,
Or that I could have had enough courage to see what I was doing to us both.

Is it enough that I recognize it now?
Can you find the grace within to forgive me,
Knowing that it will heal us both?
If you can, then we can start anew,
Even if doing so means enduring the pain I've avoided till now.

"Good morning!" Roger greeted me, pulling me back into the day. "I don't know how long I was out. Have you been awake for long?"

"I've just been doing a little writing," I replied as I placed the pad back in my bag, "and thinking about our lunch later today. Everything seems to have led to this moment."

"Everything always leads to this moment," Roger asserted as he stood up, "and that's because it's the only moment there is—right now. And right now, it's time to prepare for Alain. I don't suggest we eat beforehand, because I have the feeling he's going to go all out for us."

"What do you mean?" I asked.

"I don't know Alain very well, but I do know he's extremely generous. To him, being a chef is a way to serve, a way to make people feel joy. That's really what you and I have been talking about, isn't it? In one way or another, every conversation we've had has been about service and doing what makes your heart sing. They really are the same thing when you think about it."

"Because when you serve others, the joy you're giving always returns to you?" I asked.

"Well, hopefully yes, but it's more than that. We all need to find the one thing that makes us want to get up in the morning . . . the one thing that brings passion to our lives. When you live from that place, then your whole life is an act of service because people feel what you're doing and they instinctively want it as well. You don't get excited or energized in the morning because you have a mortgage to pay. You get excited because you've found your niche, the place where your soul thrives. Then the day goes by so fast! This is what service is for me. In my life, it's cooking fresh, high-quality food for people. And for you, it is . . ."

It seemed like an obvious answer, but even as I opened my mouth, I realized it was more complex than I anticipated.

"Well, I'm passionate about writing, and of course, my music—"

"But what is the main thing?" Roger inquired. "What is the most important thing that ties them together?"

The answer seemed obvious. "I love to empower people," I replied.

"Empower them to do what?"

"Whether I'm writing or performing a concert, I want to inspire people to achieve their soul's desire. I want them to follow their passion and live their lives in that mind-set."

"So your passion is to help people find their passion? That's interesting . . . and I think you've answered your own question."

"What was my question?"

"You want to know how you can offer yourself in service to those who are searching for love," Roger replied confidently. "Aren't love and passion the same thing? When you think about it, what you want and what you're most passionate about sharing are identical. That's going to make things much easier for you, I believe."

"But like you said or I said . . . it's what I'm already doing. It's just a matter of where I'm going to do it, or whom I'll be serving."

"You shouldn't worry about those things," Roger remarked. "Just open your heart and do it. When I'm preparing a meal, I don't wonder about the people I'm cooking for. I don't look out from the kitchen and think, *That person looks okay, but that other person doesn't.* I'm just grateful there are people in my dining room! Then I do the best job I can.

"When you think about it, God is the same. He doesn't give only to those who are 'good' or 'worthy.' God's blessings flow to all of us, just as the sun shines on everyone in the world. We can block the sun if we choose to, but that doesn't change how the gift was offered. Do you understand what I'm saying?"

"I think you're saying that it doesn't matter whether I'm writing a book or playing my guitar in front of an audience . . . the ultimate purpose is the same. I think I just need direction now."

"As soon as you put your rudder in the water, then you'll know which direction to take," Roger replied in a cryptic voice.

"My rudder?"

"Yes. When a boat has its rudder up, it can't be steered back to shore or wherever you want it to go. Imagine that your boat is engulfed in fog and you can't see the horizon or anything else in front of you, for that matter. Where do you go? What do you do? Well, the first thing you need to do is to ask for help. Maybe you have a radio and you call for directions. The point is that help is always available, but you must ask for it.

"Then once you do, you place the rudder back in the water and begin to move in the right direction. And this is what's happening for you, right? You've been asking for help and it has arrived. And it isn't just me helping you with my stories. Alice has helped you, and others have, too . . . even the ones who steered you in a different direction."

"Like Michele," I replied.

"Yes, exactly. If Michele hadn't left you on my doorstep, then we wouldn't be here right now. We wouldn't have been able to share all the things we've experienced in the last few months that have helped us both grow. That was a great gift, even though it didn't feel like it at the time."

"That's for sure," I agreed. "It definitely didn't feel like a gift at the time."

"And what does it feel like now?"

"Like a new world, I suppose. Like I'm about to walk through a gate where every possibility is opening up before me. Does that make any sense?"

"It makes more sense than you realize," Roger said, smiling. "Now let's get our coats and go see Alain. I have a feeling we're in for much more than just a wonderful lunch."

⚜⚜⚜

Alain the Great

The hotel was right around the corner from our destination: Carré des Feuillants, the famous restaurant where Alain Dutournier worked his magic. As we walked down Rue Saint-Honoré, I thought about everything that Roger and I had talked about earlier.

He was right. There were so many gifts that brought us to this moment, and I was starting to think that he knew from the very beginning where it would lead. On the one hand, Roger was a humble but supremely talented chef; on the other hand, he was one of the most fascinating mystics I'd ever met. Some artists use paint or stone as their medium, while master musicians let their brilliance speak through the instruments they play or perhaps through their own voices.

Without a doubt, Roger's instrument was food, and there were not many who could match his skills. But now we were going to meet the person Roger considered to be *his* master, someone he respected and wanted to learn from. It was as if we were embarking on an enhanced aspect of the curriculum, and I hoped I was ready for whatever might happen next.

"When I'm with Alain, I feel like an apprentice," Roger remarked as we walked.

"That's hard to believe."

"You need to know that he works with food on a very different level from most French chefs. You'll see what I mean when the dishes begin to flow. And when I say *flow,* I really mean it! I don't know how many courses there will be, but most will be tiny and delicate. This is what Alain does best. He prepares amazingly elegant food. Each bite provides an explosion of taste."

"Is Alain going to eat with us?" I asked.

"I think he'll come and join us when the meal is finished, and I'm hoping he'll take us back into the kitchen and show you around. I've been there already, and it's a kitchen I dream of at night. It is so perfect. Sometimes I feel like offering myself to him for free just so I can watch and learn."

"Would you really do that? Volunteer just to learn some of Alain's techniques? I feel like you're already a master."

"Well, I suppose, but not like Alain. I do like to fantasize about working in his kitchen. Maybe it's like you . . . I love what I'm doing with my life, but it doesn't hurt to dream."

We turned and opened two large glass doors, which seemed to lead into a hotel or elegant shopping center. In front of us I saw an enormous clay bottle, perhaps seven feet tall, and realized we had arrived. Roger led me to another glass door, and before opening it he turned and looked at me.

"Are you ready?" he asked.

He didn't wait for my answer. He swiftly opened the door and stepped inside. The small desk to the right of the door was cleared of any distractions or unnecessary papers, and as the tall man at the desk smiled at us and Roger greeted him in French, another took our coats. Then the first man escorted us into the next room, which resembled a waiting area or atrium, then into the dining room itself.

It was only 12:15 in the afternoon, and we were the first guests to arrive. The table nearest to the atrium was already set, and our host pulled out the chair for me to sit down. It was only then that I realized Roger had disappeared. I was alone in the dining room. I looked back toward the entrance and saw him speaking to a younger man in a chef's jacket. I assumed this was Alain's head chef whom Roger had mentioned, another member of the staff who had stayed at Drew House. After a few seconds, the men shook hands, and Roger turned and walked toward me, smiling broadly.

"The restaurant is much smaller than I imagined," I said to him as he took his seat.

"A place like this is never overcrowded," Roger noted. "That's one of the attractions. This is a city that honors extravagance, and there will always be customers willing to pay for it. There are not many cities in the world that can host so many incredible and expensive restaurants."

I looked around at the paintings, and the crystal vases filled with long-stemmed roses. Roger explained that the decor changed regularly; in fact, there were probably artists lined up around the block trying to get their works displayed in Alain's dining room. The waitstaff moved around us like dancers, making final preparations for a grand performance. I knew that no detail would be overlooked as one by one they arranged the stage.

Roger had just picked up the menu, as one of our many waiters appeared at the table. He began speaking in French, but after Roger spoke to him, he switched to English.

"Alain has asked me to tell you that he will be selecting your food today," he said to us. "You do not need to think about the menu at all . . . just trust the chef."

I looked at Roger. "He's going to choose everything? I feel like a celebrity."

"We are all celebrities," Roger declared. "This is just the day we get the royal treatment."

Another waiter appeared and poured us each a glass of champagne, and after Roger and I tapped glasses, I took a sip. It was open and rich, much different from any champagne I'd had in the past. I took another sip and let the fruit roll through my mouth, not wanting to miss a single flavor. Then a third waiter stepped up and presented us with a tiny ceramic plate with a petite pastry I didn't recognize.

"This is called a tartlet," Roger explained. "There is a small shrimp inside the pastry, which is meant to open your taste buds and prepare you for what is to come."

I picked up the minuscule dish, lifted it to my mouth, and let the tartlet slip inside. The texture of the dough and shrimp created a remarkable sensation, something I had never experienced before. Although it was so small and delicate, it possessed a vivacity I didn't expect. I watched Roger as he savored his tartlet, and I knew that he agreed.

"That was amazing," I remarked. "Is this how the whole meal is going to be—one miniature dish after another?"

"For the most part, yes," he said. "This is the essence of fine French dining, and it contains a great spiritual teaching as well. In other words, you don't need to have a large quantity of something for it to be worthwhile. What you need most of all is something that has a powerful essence—just like this dish. This allows the spirit to come through, not just the thing itself."

The first waiter appeared with two other small dishes. He sat them down in front of us and then smiled as if he was in on something I wasn't privy to. Roger looked down at them and grinned as well.

"Ah, you're going to love this! The first one is an asparagus mousse, which is so delicate and artistic; and the other is a single parsnip chip with horseradish cream on a boiled radish. It would be easy to be fooled by the simplicity of these dishes. I can tell you that they are so rare . . . so few restaurants have the skill to produce such delicacies."

"I don't know what I would do if you weren't here to help me," I said as I placed the mousse on my tongue. It took me several seconds to recover from the richness, which was then followed by the sensational boiled radish.

"You would have been fine," he said, "but it might have been a bit challenging. However, most, if not all, of the waiters do speak English."

"Earlier you mentioned that you thought about offering yourself to Alain as a volunteer. You didn't answer me. Would you really consider it? You're a very highly regarded chef in Canada."

"I think I would," Roger replied as he ate his mousse. "There was another great chef here in Paris I tried this with. Like Alain, he is a real master, and I thought it would be fun. I've done well for myself in Canada, but sometimes one must do things because they're enjoyable or in order to learn something new."

"Have you ever mentored someone who wanted to become a chef?"

"Many times. I love teaching young people all the things they won't learn in formal school. I love to show them about the life inside food, and that when you honor that life, it honors you. I love to show them how to buy things, because that's the thing I do best. You have to develop an eye for this, and that only comes from experience, and from being with someone who can show you how."

A different waiter stepped up to the table. "Gentlemen, I hope you're ready for another dish."

He set a slightly larger plate in front of each of us, but not much more so than the others. Once again, it was like placing a fine piece of artwork before us to enjoy.

"This is a scallop tartare with a rim of truffle and algae," the waiter explained, "on top of a curry sauce with a sliver of sesame cracker. Enjoy."

He walked away from the table, and I looked at Roger. He pointed at a small croissant-like roll, which the waiter had also placed in front of us.

"This is a fresh baguette with salted butter from Brittany," he said. "This may be the only place in Paris that serves this kind of butter. It's very expensive and really wonderful. Alain is from an area twenty miles north of where I am from. We share many of the same influences."

"You serve it as well?" I asked.

"When I can get it, yes. But this is at a very different level. I am from the Basque region, and while Alain lived only a few miles away from me, he is really more French-influenced than I am. In Basque, we would normally have bigger and fewer portions. This is the way a master like Alain prepares meals, partly because he has about forty people in the back helping him. They can afford to take the extra time to prepare the best and most elegant food."

He took a bite of the baguette, and a huge smile lit up across his face.

"This is one way that I break the rules a bit," he said. "I'm not supposed to eat wheat, but I do enjoy it when I get to do so just for a little while. I've made bread and pastries my whole life, so it's hard to give it up."

"How do you feel about giving things up?" I asked, not really knowing how to respond. "I mean, sacrificing things that you know aren't good for you?"

"That's a very good question. It's important to listen to the body when it tells you that you shouldn't eat something. At the same time, the joy it brings you may outweigh the negative effects. You can't underestimate the impact joy has on your physical and emotional body. It can transmute the ill effects and bring about greater health. It's just another reason to think of food as spiritual.

"It's not always what the doctor tells us, but also what the soul calls for. It's the same reason we sometimes bless our food before eating a meal."

We had just finished our scallop dish when the first waiter appeared again. This time he wasn't carrying anything, but I could see that there was another server right behind him who was.

"How is everything so far?" he asked. Then he turned to me. "Is this your first visit to Paris?"

"No, not my first, but I've never experienced anything quite like this."

"Ooh la la," he said with a wink, then stepped aside as the other waiter placed two plates in front of us. He looked at me first. "For you, we have squid ravioli cooked with an oyster in the middle and served with a truffle on top." Then turning to Roger he said something in French, which seemed to bring Roger great joy.

"This is really amazing," Roger said as the waiters stepped away. "Alain knows enough to give us each a dish that we will resonate with personally. He probably knows that you travel a lot, so he gave you something with a strong Asian influence. For me, he was more specific. This is a traditional Basque dish—chestnut soup with goose liver, and a tiny slice of chestnut on toast. He knew I would especially enjoy something from my native land."

"I'm not sure how many more of these I can take," I confessed. "How many courses do you think we have left?"

"It's hard to say. It seems that Alain wants to impress us, so it might go on and on."

Minutes after we finished a dish, the next soon followed. Now a completely new waiter approached our table and spoke to us in English.

"This is a black truffle made into lasagna. Alain sliced the truffle to resemble the layers of pasta. There's also a little portion of scallops, also done in layers, and a mousse of avocado with truffle."

I ate this dish in silence, letting the thin sheets of "pasta" move through my mouth, inspiring a whole new level of enjoyment. I looked over at Roger, and he seemed to be experiencing the same pleasure. He finally glanced at me and smiled.

"Do you recall what I said to you in the very beginning?" he whispered as he leaned in closer, almost as if he were about to reveal a secret. "Food is both physical and spiritual . . . do you remember? It sustains the body—that is obvious, but what it does for the soul is less noticeable.

"A great dish like this brings us to the point of utter silence, as if there is nothing else happening in the world. It carries us into the present moment like few other things can. And when we're in the present moment, then we are connecting with our soul . . . with our spirit. Do you understand what I mean? It can be like going into a great cathedral or sitting in deep meditation. If food can bring you into the Now, then it is a spiritual experience."

I wanted to say something in agreement, but two waiters appeared before I could open my mouth. One opened a bottle of red wine and poured us each a glass, and the other set dishes in front of each of us. Then he stepped back and began addressing Roger.

"This dish is a fish called turbot and is served with caviar on top as well as a broccoli emulsion." Then turning to me, he said, "And for you, sir, Alain has prepared lobster in a delicate pastry, as well as lobster asparagus with a single line of garlic sauce. Bon appétit."

"This feels a lot like being in church," I remarked before lifting the first bite to my mouth. "I feel like every cell in my body has come to life."

"I feel the same way," Roger agreed. "It's a subtle feeling but also very powerful. I believe that evolution is about becoming more and more attuned to the subtleties of life. The more aware you are of that force, which is really what allows humans to evolve, the more you see it everywhere else . . . wherever you look. True evolution is simply becoming increasingly aware of everything, especially of the things you can't see with your eyes. For me, that is the miracle of life."

Ten minutes later, we finished our fish and lobster, and no more than fifteen seconds went by before the next course was set in front of us. The two plates were concealed by bell-shaped stainless-steel covers, and when they were removed, I saw something I was unable to describe.

"Gentlemen, this is goose liver with a large truffle on top. Would you like me to add shavings from another truffle? It is recommended."

I looked at Roger and he smiled, giving me the go-ahead. The waiter produced a tool that shaved fine shreds of the mushroom, and then he gently placed them onto the goose liver. He did the same for Roger and stepped away from the table.

"I'm serious," I said to Roger. "I'm starting to get overwhelmed. It's not that I don't want more, because I'm loving this, but it eventually becomes more difficult to fully appreciate."

"It goes back to what I was saying before about evolution," Roger noted. "Too much of anything and you begin to lose the original impact. Imagine if you went to a museum such as the Louvre, right around the corner. Some of the greatest paintings in the world are there, and when you begin walking from room to room, you absorb the beauty and richness of the art with every ounce of your being.

"After a while, however, your senses grow sluggish, and you can't see as much. By the time you get to the *Mona Lisa,* she's just a reasonably attractive woman with a cheeky smile. The same applies to a meal like this. After so many dishes, your taste buds begin to shut down, and you can't enjoy it as much as before.

"Sometimes it's best to have only two or three dishes like these." Then he took a bite of the goose liver and smiled. "But then again, occasional hedonism does have its benefits."

"I have to agree," I said as I took another bite. "How often do I get the chance to eat like this? Never! I may as well put up with it and not complain."

Minutes later the first waiter stepped up to the table holding a large white cube. I wondered what it was . . . was it even food? It looked like a ceramic or clay sculpture at first, and in seconds my suspicions were confirmed. He took a small tool and broke the cube open, which turned out to be clay in which the contents had been cooked. Then the waiter began separating what looked like meat and vegetables from the clay.

"And now that we have separated the lamb and vegetables, we will take the dish back to the kitchen to finish its preparation."

He picked up the silver tray and stepped away from the table.

"So he came here just to give us the experience of breaking the clay?" I asked. "That's amazing."

"A restaurant such as this is almost like going to the theater," Roger explained. "It is as much about the show as it is the food. You probably also noticed how skillful the waiters are. They are the actors. They move about playing their parts, but they never overact. They're right where they need to be, but never seem to be in the way."

The waiter returned and placed the beautifully displayed dishes in front of us, and stepped away. I could see what Roger meant. There must have been three to four waiters serving each table, yet every aspect of our service was flawless, perfectly choreographed, as if Roger and I were the only ones there.

"I'm remembering something I did when I was in college," I remarked as we ate. "I was working for the student newspaper and had this idea to write reviews for the best restaurants in Chicago. It was really just a way to eat for free and bring a different date with me every time. The funny thing is that these weren't even the types of restaurants a student could afford . . . places like the famous Pump Room, which was frequented by celebrities. But they still let me come and eat whatever I wanted for free! I did it for weeks and wrote reviews for each one, which were published in the paper. I really can't believe I got away with it."

"Well, you got away with it because you were thinking outside the box," Roger pointed out. "It may have been a strange idea, but it was original. Never underestimate the impact of an original idea. It also prepared you for what you've been doing with your life ever since."

"How is that?" I asked.

"How many times have you thought of something so original that everyone just said *yes* and went along? Look at what we're doing right now! This really isn't any different from what you did when you were in school. And you even talked me into coming with you . . . flying across the Atlantic Ocean just to have lunch! It was all the result of an idea that had power."

"Just to have lunch," I repeated. "How do you measure something like that . . . or like this?"

The waiter appeared again as I finished speaking, and I felt a strange combination of elation and dismay.

"Lamb from the Pyrenees," he explained. "I could tell how much you liked the lamb we just served and felt you needed one more. As you can see, these are tiny lamb chops with a single bone to remind you of what you are eating. On the side, there is flan with watercress and parsley. Enjoy."

"This has to be near the end," I said. "When they begin serving the same meat, then surely there's light at the end of the tunnel."

"I think you may be right," Roger agreed. "I don't know if you noticed, but we were the first to arrive to the restaurant, and now there are only a few tables still eating. We've been here for almost three hours."

I looked at my watch and saw that he was right. The time was flying by faster than I realized, and even though we'd gone through more courses than I could count, it felt as if we hadn't been there very long at all. I took a sip of my wine and looked around again. It was as if we were in a different world, and I knew that sensation wasn't far from the truth.

For some it was a world they inhabited regularly, especially if they lived in Paris, but for me, it was as if I were being given a glimpse into a way of living I hardly knew existed. The food itself was part of the experience, but only indirectly. It was the magical nature of the moment that struck me and settled like roots into my consciousness. It was more about the opportunity to see life in a new way. I had no interest in eating like this too often, but it was accompanied by a heightened awareness I'd never known before, and it was this more than anything else that I wanted to savor.

Minutes later an enormous selection of cheeses was wheeled to our table, and after choosing two or three, the waiter precisely sliced each one and left again. Dessert soon followed: a dark-cocoa base with a white-cocoa ball covered with warm green tea, and topped off with a 1992 Armagnac, which is a type of cognac from a town called Condom in southwestern France. The heat it created inside me was like a fire that melted every other dish and taste that preceded it, merging them together into a well-orchestrated symphony of culinary delight.

I was enjoying the sensation when I looked behind Roger and saw a man with a beard walk into the dining room and glance around. When he saw us, he turned and walked toward our table. I knew immediately that this was Alain.

Roger turned and saw him, then stood up and gave Alain a hug. He was smaller than I expected, but he also projected an air of authority that I could feel even before he got to our table. He and Roger spoke in French for a moment.

"Alain, this is my friend James Twyman," Roger told him. "He is the writer I told you about in my letter. He's been learning all about French cooking and felt he needed to meet you. It may be because I spoke of you so highly myself."

Alain sat down at the table between us and looked deeply into my eyes. At first I wasn't sure what he was doing, or if he was waiting for me to say something, but then I had the sensation that he was looking *through* me rather than *at* me. The effect was stimulating, and I almost interrupted it by speaking.

"And why would you come so far to have a single lunch?" he asked before I ruined the moment. His English was slow and halting, but once again, I felt a presence that was riveting.

"That's a hard question to answer," I replied. "When I met Roger, my life began to change. It wasn't just about the food but life itself. Then he told me about you, specifically about the time you stayed at Drew House."

"Ah yes." Alain nodded, smiling, then looked at Roger. "That is when I met this man and his lovely wife."

"Roger told me some interesting stories, and after some time, I felt that I needed to meet you in person."

"Which stories?" Alain asked.

"To begin, Roger told me what you would choose for your last meal . . . that is, what you would have if it was your last meal on Earth."

Alain seemed to know exactly what I meant, and a warm smile spread across his face. "Fried eggs! Yes, I do remember."

"When I heard that story, I knew there was a lesson there," I continued. "I realized that you understood something about life that transcended food—and I wanted to learn it."

"But what can you learn from this?" he asked. "It is such a simple thing, something from my heart. I didn't care about having a fancy meal. I can have that every day. I craved something that reminded me of my mother; I wanted to relive the way she would cook for me."

"Exactly. You didn't care about having an extravagant, decadent meal. You wanted something ordinary—something from your youth. It made me realize that abundance isn't about having *more* of something, but the essence of something that is deeper and more meaningful."

"What does abundance mean?" he asked Roger.

"Abundance can mean many things," he replied. "To some people, it means having lots of money. To me, those individuals are poor even though they seem to be rich. I believe that what James is saying is that you understood what *real* abundance was."

"Yes, yes, I understand," Alain said, suddenly excited. "You are saying that it comes from the heart, not the wallet. If abundance does not bring joy that spills over to others, then it really is nothing. That is why I wanted the fried eggs—because I knew it would make me feel happy. Not just an ordinary happiness, but one that would touch others."

"Roger also told me how you wouldn't accept a fee from the man who invited you to Canada to prepare the dinner for charity," I said. "All you wanted was to taste the wines he served. Once again, it struck me very deeply. It reminded me that money is nothing if you don't have what makes your heart sing. For you, that was being able to taste wine you had never experienced before."

"And Alain is someone who knows great wine," Roger added. "That meant he was able to appreciate what was there, which is another great lesson. *Appreciation.*"

"Can you repeat that? I'm so sorry, but my English is not so good," Alain said, looking to Roger. The two of them began speaking in French for a moment, and seconds later I could tell that he made the connection.

"Yes," Alain agreed. "I was able to understand what was there, and it was more important to me than the money. What I wanted was the experience—to appreciate the experience."

"It was a great lesson for me," I noted, "and it makes me want to ask you another question, probably the most important one. It's something that has been with me ever since I met Roger." I paused just long enough to let enough space fill the moment. This had been in my mind for months, and I had the feeling Alain was the one who would answer it. "Can you tell me why you think food is spiritual?"

It seemed like a simple, even obvious, question given the moment, but it really was the essence of everything I had learned or wanted to learn up to that point. Through Roger, I was able to see food and dining in a new way, and I felt that Alain would appreciate this more than anyone else.

"You have to think about it like this," he began. "In the very beginning, when we were living in caves and didn't know much about food, we ate what we needed to survive. In other words, it was very basic. We would kill something and we would cook it, or maybe not cook it at all, and we would eat it without thinking. This went on for a very, very long time . . . perhaps thousands of years.

"But then something interesting happened. It was probably when the women in the village began to think of food as something they could use to show their love. They realized that with a little creativity, they could do something different . . . and it made people happy. Their families felt the love that went into the food, and they enjoyed it so much more. Of course, this made the women want to get even more creative, and they found even more new ways to prepare the food, use spices, or do whatever else they had at the time. Soon they began to develop recipes, and food changed. But it changed because of the women's love—because they wanted to share their love with others. This is why it is so spiritual to me. It is a way to share love, and when you do so, it connects with the soul."

"So the love the people felt made the women seek new ways to share their love," I reflected. "In other words, the love itself began to spiral outward."

"That's it," Alain agreed, smiling. "It began to spiral out, to become more tangible and more integrated into the food itself. In the end, *food is love and love is food*. I don't think I can describe it any better."

"How do we get back to thinking of it in that way?" I asked. "For most people, there is no love in food. They consume things that hurt their bodies and don't think of the experience of eating as something healing. I know that the food you create is much different."

"The food I create comes from many places," Alain remarked. "But it mainly comes from the people who have loved me. It's my duty, my honor, to give that love away to others. As far as getting back to this way of thinking . . . well, I think that love always finds its own way.

"I can't figure that out with just my mind because, like Roger, I'm a simple cook. Maybe people think I'm a big shot here in Paris, but at the root, I am just a cook. All I can do is live this philosophy and share it with men and women like you. Maybe you will write a book that will share this idea in a new way, and maybe people will begin to understand."

Alain seemed to think about something that shifted his attention. "Please . . . come with me. There's something I want to show you."

He stood up, and Roger and I followed. Alain led us through the atrium and straight into the kitchen. We passed five or so people who were cleaning or preparing things for the meals they would serve later that night, and continued to a small stairwell that was dark at the bottom. Alain stopped at the top and pointed to a very large photograph on the wall. It seemed to be a reenactment of da Vinci's *Last Supper,* but with a modern flare. He spoke to Roger in French, who then translated for me.

"This was a photo that appeared in a well-known French magazine many years ago," Roger said. "It shows the most famous chefs in Paris as if they were at the Last Supper. These men pictured here are the superstars of haute cuisine . . . so it's funny for me to see."

"Is Alain in the photo?" I asked.

"Yes, I am," he said, pointing at the far left side of the table. "This is me when I was very young. Look, I even have the same beard."

I looked back and forth a couple of times to see how he had changed. Although many years had obviously passed since the picture had been taken, Alain still possessed the same glimmer in his eyes, the very one I was seeing at this moment.

"Every meal is the Last Supper," he asserted. "If every meal is considered as sacred as this, then it touches the soul and sparks our love. And this is why it is spiritual. Jesus knew what he was doing when he decided to teach this lesson around a table. Food isn't just something for our bodies. If it comes from our desire to love one another, then it's like communion. It gives us spiritual life.

"If I can remember that when I'm in this kitchen cooking for whoever walks through my door, then I will have accomplished what I am here on Earth to do. That is the only thing that is important to me."

I looked at Roger and smiled, and he offered a knowing grin. Standing there in the kitchen of one of the most famous chefs in the world, I was finally beginning to understand. In that moment, I would have given anything for a plate of fried eggs.

CHAPTER THIRTEEN

The Light Comes

We left the restaurant and began walking in the direction of the Louvre, then to the Jardin des Tuileries, the park that runs along the Seine from the museum to the Luxor Obelisk. It was a clear, warm day considering it was early January; and I felt light-headed as we walked.

I looked over at Roger, who had a wide smile stretched across his face, which conveyed the contentment you feel when you reach the end of an important journey and realize that everything has unfolded perfectly. I wasn't sure if my original plan included anything I had actually experienced, especially meeting Alain, but it was enough to remind me just how amazing life can be when you open yourself up and live in the moment.

It was only then that I acknowledged that this story was coming to an end, at least this particular chapter, and it filled me with a strange mixture of joy and concern—joy because so much had shifted in my life since meeting Roger, and concern because it felt as if everything was about to change again. There was no way to know what that meant or where it would lead, but I felt genuinely happy to have made it so far in such a short period of time.

We stopped by a large pool with a fountain not far from the Obelisk. Several children were operating remote-controlled sailboats while tourists and locals watched. Roger looked over at me as if he wanted to say something but wasn't quite sure how to begin. So much had happened since our first days together, and although it felt as if we had been through so much, I also knew that I hardly knew him. He was like a character that shows up and changes everything before slipping back into the ether. I was glad that Roger found me and took me under his wing, and at the same time, I sincerely hoped our friendship would continue.

"There are two final things I want to talk to you about," Roger finally stated as we started walking again. "The first has to do with food, and the second has to do with love, which I believe is your next step."

"My next step? Do you mean—"

"That you're ready to take a step you've been afraid to take? Yes, that is exactly what I mean. It may be next week or it may be next year. The time isn't important—only your readiness. This is why you landed on my doorstep, and it is what everything has led us to. The meal with Alain was like a celebratory feast, especially since he didn't even charge us."

"That was an amazing gift," I agreed. "He is as generous as you said he was."

"It's not every day two people fly from North America just to have lunch at his restaurant. Anyway, I want to make sure you notice that the final step is right in front of you . . . the one you've wanted to take your whole life but have been unable to do so."

"I sense that it has always been right there," I remarked, "but for some reason, I've been blind to it."

"This is precisely what I mean. You've been given opportunities with many wonderful women, none of whom you were able to see because you weren't able to see yourself. In the last few months, you've been given a glimpse of who you really are, and now that you have seen yourself, only one question remains: will you keep your eyes open, or will you shut them again?

"If you choose to keep them open, then the perfect person will find you. You won't need to find her. She'll be drawn to you because she's able to see herself, just like you are seeing yourself now. I hope what I'm saying is making sense."

"I think you're saying that I'll attract someone who is in the same place as I am," I responded.

"That's right, but before we get too far into that, I want to bring up another issue. In many ways, it's the only thing I ever talk about, especially when it comes to food. You've heard me say it over and over—that it is vital to add the most important ingredient, whether you're buying vegetables or cooking or serving the final dish. The key ingredient is *love!* Eating unloved food is like living an unloved life. Do you understand what I mean by that?

"In order for the food to offer the highest benefits, it must nourish the soul as well as the body. The love you put in is something you should be conscious of at every step. When I buy the food I use in my recipes, I thank everyone who brought it to me, from the earth to the farmer, then to the people who are selling it. When I prepare and cook it, I think of the people who are going to sit at my table, and I send loving thoughts to them. And who do you think benefits the most from this way of thinking?"

"I'm going to guess that *you* do," I said, knowing exactly where Roger was leading me.

"Of course! The love goes into my heart, my lungs, every part of me . . . and then it flows to Kathleen and to you and to everyone else I come in contact with. This is my way to serve others, as well as myself. It is the same thing when you think about it."

"I really like what you said about eating unloved food being like living an unloved life," I told him. "I've always considered myself a loving person, but I'm beginning to see how I've held back from the one who needs it most."

"By withholding love from yourself, you become trapped in ways you can never understand with your brain. That's because love doesn't come from the intellect. It is something that can only be comprehended by the heart and soul. And what do you think happens when you focus there, instead of the parts of you that don't understand?"

"You connect with the heart and soul of others," I said confidently as I suddenly stopped walking. It was as if the tumblers were falling into place, and I was finally getting everything that Roger was saying to me—not only in that moment but from the very beginning. "This is what true service is—not just what you do with your body, but what you do within yourself, which connects with the deepest part of everyone else."

"Now you will be a great chef!" Roger declared with a smile bigger than I had ever seen before. "You still might not know everything about cooking, but you do know the most important thing I can teach. This, at least to me, is the secret and the art of French cuisine: to nourish people from the inside out. As Alain said, this is what makes us different from our ancestors who lived thousands of years ago—our ability to serve others through our love. What we offer to others, we in turn offer to ourselves. In the end, it is the same thing."

As the words came out of Roger's mouth, I suddenly knew what I had to do . . . the service that would help heal the part of me that didn't feel like it deserved to be loved, and at the same time, also help heal all the women who had been hurt by me (and men just like me). I intuitively knew that it wouldn't just be the handful of women I'd encountered in my life, but women from around the world who were ready to be empowered by men who are finally willing to ask for forgiveness just as I was.

I realized that men and women needed each other to be whole, and that together we form a circle of healing energy that sweeps across the planet. But it has to start with the men . . . of that I was sure, and for that to happen, it had to start with me. And I was ready to begin.

"I know what I need to do," I told Roger. "I can't explain why, but it's crystal clear to me now. I mentioned earlier that I've been writing something called 'Sister, Forgive Me,' but now I see that it isn't meant to be just a poem or perhaps even a book. It's a movement!

"Imagine what would happen if all men and women made the commitment to heal themselves by offering healing to those in their lives they've wounded over the years. It starts with one person, but then it grows and becomes so much more because it's something we all need. I'm not the only one! Nearly all of us have been where I've been and done many of the thoughtless things I've done. If we can admit our mistakes and support each other, then we all benefit. Does that make any sense at all?"

"Yes, I think it does," Roger replied. "But what exactly are you thinking of doing?"

"I know exactly what I'm going to do!" It was as if I could see the entire thing right in front of me. "I'm going to create a website where men can go and record their own version of 'Sister, Forgive Me.' Maybe they'll write their own stories or poems, or perhaps they'll record something that expresses what they feel. Then women will come to the site to read or listen to the entries, and when they do, they'll feel the energy that all those men are releasing. It can offer profound healing. Women can also go there to share the ways they've hurt the men in their lives. It will serve as a portal where people can lay their feelings right on the table and know that they're being used to heal others as well as themselves."

"I've never heard of anything like that before," Roger remarked. "This has a very special place in my heart. The Divine feminine has always been revered here in France, especially in the south, but for more than two thousand years, this powerful energy has been buried and ignored. Even condemned! It's the exact thing that men have done to the female spirit whenever they make women feel as if they are less than they are. And even though times have changed in the last hundred years or so, it is very deep in the human con-sciousness. What you're suggesting might offer a way to release it once and for all, but only if enough people take the challenge."

"That has to be my goal, then. I need to inspire men to step forward and play their own unique role. I was assuming that my service needed to focus on women, but it's starting to look like it's for men."

"It is for both!" Roger was clearly caught up in my excitement. "That is what makes it so special. And imagine, it all came from a few cloves of garlic being smashed on my cutting board."

"It started with me being abandoned on your doorstep, and now here we are in Paris . . . and everything seems to make per-fect sense. Do you believe that things sometimes happen, even if they're uncomfortable or difficult, in order to get us to the point where we can inspire and help many more people? I think that's what is happening here."

Roger stopped in his path and looked deeply into my eyes.

"James, I knew that was happening the first moment I saw you standing in the driveway. Do you remember when I told you that the produce speaks to me when I'm at the market? The same thing applies to people. Our souls speak to one another all the time, and when I listened to yours, I heard two things.

"First of all, I heard that you were ready. Second, I sensed that the healing you desired would only come through helping others . . . especially in healing the same thing you've been struggling with: *intimacy*. I felt it that first morning, and now you've felt it for yourself. And what a beautiful place to experience it—in Paris, the city of lovers."

I looked around where we were standing and smiled as I spotted at least five couples walking through the park hand in hand, or sitting on park benches kissing. Love was all around me, and for the first time, my eyes were wide open.

Not only was I surrounded by love, but I felt it within me as well. The feeling of vulnerability that had once overwhelmed me now seemed like a precious gift, something I wanted to hold on to for the rest of my life. I realized that feeling *safe* doesn't mean keeping my distance from the things that might hurt me. I had to keep my heart open, knowing that I possessed the strength within to overcome any obstacles.

The things that wound us sometimes become our greatest teachers—showing us ways that we can best serve the world. It was all right in front of me, just as it had always been, but for the first time, I could clearly see.

The next morning, Roger left without even waking me up. He had an early flight back to Toronto and snuck out so quietly that part of me wondered if he had been there at all. He'd had such a profound effect on so many areas of my life, and I was filled with gratitude.

Most important, I felt ready to experience a new level of love and intimacy. I had been thinking about the website and movement I'd talked to Roger about the day before, and it was thrilling.

All of my ideas were as strong and vibrant as ever—even more so. But there was one last thing I had to do before I could step forward into such an enormous venture . . . there was one last section of the poem to write, one last gift to every woman who had entered my life, as well as women everywhere who had been wounded by the men in their lives. Then I would be ready, and I knew that nothing would stop me.

I sat down on the bed with the pad of paper, picked up my pen, and began to write:

Sister, it feels like I've turned a corner,
One that I didn't know existed a moment ago.

Were you the one who inspired this movement?
Or was it something neither of us could have seen before now,
Deeper than our breath or the wounds that have driven us into the shadows
Where we hid unannounced?

A seed that was buried breaks through the surface of our lives,
And as we stretch toward the sun with our hands and hearts open wide
We renew our commitment to love and to each other.
It took us this long to finally arrive at this place,
And now that we're here, I reach my hand toward yours and we step forward—
Into a world we have yet to create.

It's as if I've opened my eyes for the first time,
And I can see you looking at me,
Vulnerable and awake.

How could we have understood the changes taking place within us?
Who was there to witness the beautiful opening of our lives?

A light begins to expand inside our hearts,
Filling us with more energy than we've ever known before.
Is it possible that this is what we've been waiting for?
Was this the promise we sensed even when we stood in the shadows,
Waiting for the sudden approach of heaven?

All I know is that I can no longer remain where I once stood,
As if one door has opened and the other suddenly disappears.

I've tried to stand still, hoping to delay the step that appears before me now,
But then I remember why I came—
Not to vanish, but to forgive;
Not to abandon, but to absolve the restless spirit that has claimed me till now.

Thank you for the persistent echo that moves through me still.
Thank you for reminding me that yesterday has been abandoned,
And tomorrow is nothing more than a mist that fades as the sun rises.

I am ready to stand in front of you without running,
I am ready to hold you instead of moving.
I am ready to hold myself without worrying about who is looking.
I am here, present and whole—perhaps for the first time,
All because I was willing to look inside both of our hearts,
And not recoil when the thunder shook the air around our bodies.

Thank you, dearest Sister, for holding me accountable for everything I am,
And everything I might become.
It is the only thing that is left of me now,
And time won't forget this moment of perfect grace.

I called Michele two months later. As I waited for her to answer, I wondered how I would explain everything that had happened. I was no longer the indecisive man who ran away from love just as quickly as I ran toward it.

I was crushed but was then reborn, and now that life coursed through my soul again, all I wanted to do was look forward. And yet there was something I had to say to Michele, even if it was just for my own healing. If she didn't understand or accept what I had to offer, I still needed to say the words.

I heard her voice, which pulled me back into the moment: *"Hi, this is Michele. I can't get to the phone right now, but if you leave your name and the time you called, I'll get back to you as soon as I can."* When I heard the beep, I paused, not sure if I should leave a message or call back later. By then at least three seconds of silence had passed, and I figured I should say something.

"Hi Michele, it's James. You're probably really surprised to hear from me again. I guess I'm kind of surprised, too. I just wanted to call and tell you something that's—"

I heard a click and realized I was no longer being recorded. It never occurred to me that she had an actual answering machine, the kind you could interrupt if you really did want to talk to the person after you figured out who it was or heard what they had to say. At first I didn't hear anything other than her breath, but then the voice I remembered spoke.

"Wow. This is a call I didn't think I would ever get. I figured you'd moved on to someone else you could overwhelm with your charm and wit. It never occurred to me that you'd keep my number."

I took a deep breath before replying, wondering if I'd made a mistake in calling her. The journey I had been on actually had very little to do with Michele and the specific details of our relationship. It was so much bigger than one woman, but encompassed every relationship I had ever been a part of, and would ever be a part of. More than anything, it was about my own life and fears, as well as the healing that seemed to have taken place.

And yet Michele *did* play an important role. She was the initiator who'd pointed me in the right direction, then kicked me in the ass to get me moving. Lucky for me, she had done it in the driveway of a master chef who understood the key to happiness. I realized that I owed her for that, whether Michele knew it or not.

"Of course I still have your number," I replied. "You've been on my mind a lot lately . . . more than you realize."

"I wondered if it would happen: you calling me up, saying you're in Toronto, and that you want to get together to talk. How far away are you?"

"Really far. I'm back in Oregon. I wish I could stop by, but it's a long drive."

"Okay," she said after pausing long enough to recalibrate. "Then what's up? You haven't called in months—not even an e-mail. Why the sudden interest?"

"Well, there are a lot of reasons. Pretty big reasons, actually . . . but they only involve you indirectly."

"Indirectly?"

"Both indirectly and directly, I guess. I know we haven't spoken since I was at Drew House, which ended up changing my life. I guess being left in an unfamiliar place where you don't know anyone has its benefits. . . ."

"I'm glad there was a silver lining," she responded in a way that was impossible to gauge.

"More than you can understand," I continued. "Roger, the chef who owns Drew House, and I have become very close. We've had a couple of amazing adventures together. Do you believe we went all the way to Paris just to have lunch?"

I could feel the shift even before she said anything. The shock of my call combined with the transformation that had occurred was more than she expected, or wanted, to hear. Part of me wanted to say a quick thank-you and get off the phone, but the other part knew that I had to wait, to listen to her words and embrace them. It was my first real test, and I wanted to pass it.

"What do you think you're doing right now?" she asked. "You call me after months of no contact to tell me that you had lunch in Paris? How am I supposed to respond to that? What do you want from me?"

"I'm sorry, Michele . . . but there's something else that you deserve to hear. Everything that happened since you left created a space inside me. I've been filling it with all the things I had been unable, or even unwilling, to receive until now. You were a big part of that shift, and I thought you deserved to know it."

"So you want me to know that leaving you in Elora changed your life? That's great, James. I'm really happy for you. It's not every day a girl hears that she played such a positive role in a man's life."

"There's more," I said, trying to soften the tension between us. "I've been working on something—kind of a poem, I guess. I thought I would send it to you, but it would be better if you heard it directly from me, even if it's over the phone. It's what I learned during this period, as well as where I'm heading. If it's okay, I was hoping you would let me read some of it to you. . . ."

There was a long silence, and I knew she was trying to decide what to do. I wouldn't have blamed her if she said no—that it didn't make any sense to let me back into her life, even if it was just long enough to listen to a poem written by a man she thought she would never hear from again. I finally heard her take a deep breath, as if she were preparing herself for whatever came next.

"All right. Fine. Go ahead and read me your poem."

"You need to know that it's not only to you, but to every woman I've ever been with, or who I might encounter in the future. It's a way of seeing past appearances to what is genuine. I realized that every woman is my sister, just as every man is my brother, and that has changed everything."

I started to read, beginning with the title, "Sister, Forgive Me." I read it slowly and with as much feeling as I could convey. The other end of the line was so quiet that I wondered if Michele had hung up. Then I heard a sound, at first indistinct, but it didn't take long for me to realize that she was softly crying. I continued reading until I was finished, then paused, hoping she would respond.

"That was beautiful," Michele said. "Really . . . that was one of the most beautiful things I've ever heard."

"Really? Did it make sense to you?"

"Of course. It really touched my heart, James. Do you realize that those are the words every woman wants to hear? I can imagine how it must have made you feel. Think of the healing if every man had the chance to do something similar, to share from his heart and learn from his mistakes. I see what you mean when you said that the poem wasn't just for us. It's for everyone who has been wounded by love."

"Men and women," I added.

"Yes, you're right. Women have done the exact same thing to men. I feel like you've opened a door—and now anyone can walk through it . . . just like we did."

"So where do we go from here?" I asked her.

"Do you mean us, or everyone? I have no idea where you and I will go, but you need to do whatever you can to share what you've written. Hearing those words almost makes me glad I left you standing there in the driveway."

Michele and I continued talking for at least an hour that day, sharing stories and catching up on the details of our lives. By the time we were ready to hang up, I felt as if a heavy weight had been lifted. I felt lighter, ready to step into a life I had only imagined before. There was no way to know what that meant or where it might lead, but I felt prepared . . . and I knew that love would surely follow.

"If you create the space for love, then love will always enter," I recalled Roger telling me once. "If there's one thing God doesn't like, it's an empty, unfilled space in your heart."

He was right.

Afterword

When I first told Roger that I was going to write a book about our friendship and everything I had learned from him, he seemed nervous and slightly overwhelmed. I don't think he likes being viewed as anything other than an ordinary chef, certainly not the wise master he has proven himself to be in my own life. Many of the things he's shared with me and which I wrote about in this book were from recordings I made during our conversations, while others were painted with broader strokes based on the interactions and chats we had.

The fact that Roger sees himself in a different light just adds fuel to what I perceive as the truth: he is one of those rare individuals who doesn't need fame or public recognition to determine who he is. I suppose he's right to believe that, and I know that I'm right in my assessment of him as well. He came into my life and helped me see things I had been blind to, and for me that's proof enough.

Having written many books on a variety of spiritual topics, I believe that we need more teachers like Roger Dufau. Over the last fifteen years, I've spoken at nearly every spiritual conference and expo that exists, and I've met almost every well-known teacher. Because of those experiences, I feel like I've learned a few important lessons.

There are some teachers I know who remind me why I've chosen this work; they inspire me to continue. In other words, I see qualities in them that I wish to emulate. On the other hand, there are others who have taught me a very different lesson—the exact opposite, in fact. These are the individuals who seem more concerned with their public persona than in sharing the truth in ways that are uniquely their own. Their focus is on achieving fame, and it seems that many of them have lost sight of why they stepped onto this path in the first place.

It's certainly not my place to judge, but it *is* up to me to choose the people I hope to emulate and learn from. It's also up to me to compassionately view and try to understand the behaviors I don't want to reproduce. That's what will make me even more effective in sharing the messages I'm so passionate about.

Roger is one of the people I will emulate. His humility is one of his greatest qualities, and I don't think he'll ever lose it. Not only that, but the guy can cook . . . my goodness, better than anyone I've ever met! His spirituality is wrapped tightly in the recipes and techniques that have made him a master chef, and it is there that he shines brightest.

If you're ever near Toronto and have a couple of days free, consider making the drive to Elora so you can see for yourself. I promise you won't be disappointed. In fact, I truly believe that after only a few minutes, you'll turn to the person you're with and say, "This guy is exactly how James described him!" That would make me smile.

Incidentally, just to prove this, Roger and I recently shot a series of short cooking classes that can be found on YouTube via the Hay House channel (**www.youtube.com/hayhousepresents**). Check them out, and get ready to learn from the master!

As for my own life since this experience . . . well, let's just say that it's unfolding nicely. The lessons I learned from Roger and Alain have taken root and are manifesting in all sorts of incredible ways. I know that my heart is open, and that I'll attract the right person at the right time. For now, I'm content to wait and not rush the process.

The key is that I've finally fallen in love with the most important person: *myself.* From there, love will blossom and expand, all because of that fateful day in Elora and the lonely driveway that changed my life.

I'll keep you posted.

⚜ ⚜ ⚜

ABOUT THE AUTHOR

 **James F. Twyman** is the bestselling author of numerous books, including *The Barn Dance* and *The Moses Code*. He is an internationally renowned 'Peace Troubadour' who has a reputation for drawing millions of people together in prayer to positively influence crises throughout the world. He has been invited by leaders of countries such as Iraq, Northern Ireland, South Africa, Bosnia, Croatia and Serbia to perform The Peace Concert – often while conflicts raged in those areas; and he has performed at the United Nations, the Pentagon, and more.

James is the executive producer and co-writer of the feature film *Indigo*, and the director of *Indigo Evolution* and the documentary *The Moses Code*. He is also the founder of The Seminary of Spiritual Peacemaking, which has ordained over 500 ministers from around the world.

www.jamestwyman.com

Notes

Notes

Notes

Notes

Notes

Notes

Hay House Titles of Related Interest

YOU CAN HEAL YOUR LIFE: *the movie,* starring Louise L. Hay &
Friends (available as a 1-DVD program and an expanded 2-DVD set)
Watch the trailer at: **www.LouiseHayMovie.com**

***THE SHIFT, the movie,* starring Dr. Wayne W. Dyer** (available as a
1-DVD program and an expanded 2-DVD set)
Watch the trailer at: **www.DyerMovie.com**

*AM I BEING KIND: How Asking One Simple Question Can
Change Your Life . . . and Your World,* by Michael J. Chase

THE MAP: Finding the Magic and Meaning in the Story of Your Life,
by Colette Baron-Reid

*MARRIED TO BHUTAN: How One Woman Got Lost, Said "I Do,"
and Found Bliss,* by Linda Leaming

*THE POWER OF INFINITE LOVE & GRATITUDE: An Evolutionary
Journey to Awakening Your Spirit,* by Dr. Darren R. Weissman

TRAVELLING AT THE SPEED OF LOVE, by Sonia Choquette

YOU CAN CREATE AN EXCEPTIONAL LIFE,
by Louise Hay and Cheryl Richardson

All of the above are available at your local bookstore,
or may be ordered by contacting Hay House (see next page).

We hope you enjoyed this Hay House book.
If you would like to receive a free catalogue featuring additional
Hay House books and products, or if you would like information
about the Hay Foundation, please contact:

Hay House UK Ltd
292B Kensal Road • London W10 5BE
Tel: (44) 20 8962 1230; Fax: (44) 20 8962 1239
www.hayhouse.co.uk

***

Published and distributed in the United States of America by:
Hay House, Inc. • PO Box 5100 • Carlsbad, CA 92018-5100
Tel: (1) 760 431 7695 or (1) 800 654 5126;
Fax: (1) 760 431 6948 or (1) 800 650 5115
www.hayhouse.com

***

Published and distributed in Australia by:
Hay House Australia Ltd • 18/36 Ralph Street • Alexandria, NSW 2015
Tel: (61) 2 9669 4299, Fax: (61) 2 9669 4144
www.hayhouse.com.au

***

Published and distributed in the Republic of South Africa by:
Hay House SA (Pty) Ltd • PO Box 990 • Witkoppen 2068
Tel/Fax: (27) 11 467 8904
www.hayhouse.co.za

***

Published and distributed in India by:
Hay House Publishers India • Muskaan Complex • Plot No.3
B-2 • Vasant Kunj • New Delhi - 110 070
Tel: (91) 11 41761620; Fax: (91) 11 41761630
www.hayhouse.co.in

***

Distributed in Canada by:
Raincoast • 9050 Shaughnessy St • Vancouver, BC V6P 6E5
Tel: (1) 604 323 7100
Fax: (1) 604 323 2600

***

Sign up via the Hay House UK website to receive the Hay House
online newsletter and stay informed about what's going on with your
favourite authors. You'll receive bimonthly announcements
about discounts and offers, special events, product highlights,
free excerpts, giveaways, and more!
www.hayhouse.co.uk

JOIN THE HAY HOUSE FAMILY

As the leading self-help, mind, body and spirit publisher in the UK, we'd like to welcome you to our family so that you can enjoy all the benefits our website has to offer.

 **EXTRACTS** from a selection of your favourite author titles

 **COMPETITIONS, PRIZES & SPECIAL OFFERS** Win extracts, money off, downloads and so much more

 **LISTEN** to a range of radio interviews and our latest audio publications

 **CELEBRATE YOUR BIRTHDAY** An inspiring gift will be sent your way

 **LATEST NEWS** Keep up with the latest news from and about our authors

 **ATTEND OUR AUTHOR EVENTS** Be the first to hear about our author events

 **iPHONE APPS** Download your favourite app for your iPhone

 **HAY HOUSE INFORMATION** Ask us anything, all enquiries answered

join us online at **www.hayhouse.co.uk**

 292B Kensal Road, London W10 5BE
T: 020 8962 1230 E: info@hayhouse.co.uk